Pinar Tuzcu
"Ich bin eine Kanackin"

Gender Studies

Dedicated to Joscha-Nicolai Spoellmink.
For your inspiring commitment and infectious creativity, Joscha.

Pinar Tuzcu (Dr. phil.) holds a postdoc position and teaches at the Department of Sociology of Diversity at the University of Kassel. Her research interests include contemporary feminisms and queer theory, postmigration studies, decolonial approaches and speculative methodology.

Pinar Tuzcu
"Ich bin eine Kanackin"
Decolonizing Popfeminism –
Transcultural Perspectives on Lady Bitch Ray

[transcript]

Theses completed at the University of Kassel, Faculty of Social Science. Pinar Tuzcu. The date of the viva voce: 17. June 2015

This project was funded by a three-year full scholarship from Rosa Luxemburg Foundation, Berlin.

Bibliographic information published by the Deutsche Nationalbibliothek
The Deutsche Nationalbibliothek lists this publication in the Deutsche Nationalbibliografie; detailed bibliographic data are available in the Internet at http://dnb.d-nb.de

© 2017 transcript Verlag, Bielefeld

All rights reserved. No part of this book may be reprinted or reproduced or utilized in any form or by any electronic, mechanical, or other means, now known or hereafter invented, including photocopying and recording, or in any information storage or retrieval system, without permission in writing from the publisher.

Cover layout: Kordula Röckenhaus, Bielefeld
Cover illustration: Alexander Fanslau (photographer), Lady Bitch Ray (direction)
Printed in Germany
Print-ISBN 978-3-8376-3572-0
PDF-ISBN 978-3-8394-3572-4

Table of Contents

Introduction | 7

"Ich bin 'ne Kanackin" | 29
Beyond Sexual Explicitness—Resistance Through Insistence | 31
Feminism's (M)others | 38
Kanack_in—Pluralizations and Queerings | 41
Translingualizations | 49
Productive Paradoxes | 55

Situational Analysis of the Group Discussions | 63
Situational Analysis—Maps, Gaps, and Traps | 65
    Shaping Discourses, Knitting the *Not Yet* | 67
    Linking Theoretical Sensitivity with Self-Reflexivity | 73
Grounded Theory in Multilingual Research—In-Vivo Coding and Transcultural Translation | 75
    Translanguaging the Coding Process | 77
    In-Vivo Coding—Living in Translation | 80
Situating the Group Discussions | 84
    Informant Participants—the Knowledge
    that is (not) Power | 87
    The Unsaid in the Said; The Said in the Unsaid
    —Digressions and Silences | 89
The Project Map: A Trefoil Knot | 92

Not Yet A Code—Transcultural Locational Feminism | 95
Turkishness, or Where on Earth? | 95
    "Looking one's Parents in the Eyes" | 96
    From Duisburg to Istanbul—Transcultural Geographies | 106
Germanness—the Second Person 'I' | 119
    Sexual Emancipation and Its Cultural Limits
    —*Özenti Olmak* | 119
    Almost the Same but Not Quite | 127
Feminism—Aposiopetic Positioning | 134
    Pointing at the Limits of Existing Discourses | 145
    A Question, Not Yet an Answer | 150

Conclusion | 153

Bibliography | 159
Images Cited | 189

Introduction

"What the eff," a colleague of mine muttered half-jokingly after watching Lady Bitch Ray's music video for "Du Bist Krank." Sitting in a group of five, we found ourselves googling around, digging for more information about the artist. Our debate got energized when we found out that she has Turkish cultural background and pursues an academic career. Revolving around questions of today's feminism and pop culture, the discussion awkwardly languished and stalled when it came to issues of migration and cultural difference. It was this moment that generated my interest in the central questions dealt with in this book project: How does the current form of popfeminism in Germany animate and materialize issues related to a history of migration? More specifically, how can one situate Germany's *Neuer Feminismus* in a postmigration condition? Rather than providing a single concrete answer to these questions, this study seeks to trace and map out the discursive dynamics at play in the process of relating these topics. Being guided by the discursive entanglements emerging in the group discussions I conducted, I analyze how Lady Bitch Ray's performance embodies forms of a transcultural popfeminism.

Coming from working-class parents who migrated from Sivas (Turkey) to Bremen (Germany), and having grown up in Gröpelingen, which is known as a working-class district, Reyhan Sahin became a controversial media figure with her pseudonym Lady Bitch Ray in 2006 after posting a series of porn rap songs on her MySpace site. Her refusal to remove her sexually explicit rap songs and pin-up-like images cost her her job at Radio Bremen where she was working as a radio host. Having lost this job, she created her own internet pay-per-view talk show *Kleine Fische, Große Fische*, hosting male rappers and ridiculing their glorification of hypermasculinity and misogyny by parodically reversing gender-stereotypical sexual objectification. She reached a larger audience with her role as a witty, self-assertive prostitute in Özgür Yıldırım's 2008 film *Chiko*. After the film's release she was invited to *Schmidt & Pocher*, a popular late night TV talk show. In this show, she presented her vaginal secretion in a small transparent balm container to one of the hosts. This triggered further media attention and her interviews appeared in numerous major German newspaper outlets. In response to the media's increasing interest and recurrent highlighting of her cultural background, she said in one of her early interviews with the daily boulevard paper *Bild*: "I am neither German nor Turkish; I'm a female Kanack" (Ich bin nicht Deutsch nicht Türkisch, ich bin eine Kanackin) (Lady Bitch Ray 2009).

This study focuses in depth on her feminization of the label 'Kanak'—a label which embodies processes of otherization as well as politics of resistance set in Germany's postmigration scene—and analyzes the links between contemporary popfeminist activism and politics of cultural difference. The first chapter maps out these links by focusing on Lady Bitch Ray's employment of the term *Kanackin* by drawing on her interviews and her recently published book *Bitchsm: Emanzipation, Masturbation, Integration* to situate her performance with regard to both transnational and locationally specific feminist histories. This chapter aims at illuminating the shortcomings of existing definitions of what is called *Neuer Feminismus* to expand its meaning towards notions of transculturality by referring to queer and migrant feminist histories in Germany. The second chapter elaborates on this study's use of decolonial methodologies and Situational Analysis in connection with the empirical data gathered with three group discussions. This chapter pays particular attention to the necessity of transcultural translation with respect to the participants' shifting positions in their interpretation of Lady Bitch Ray's music video. These shifting positions and the resulting discursive entanglements are the main concern of the third chapter, which presents an in-depth empirical analysis of the group discussions.

In this book, I use the term *postmigration* to describe a process of social change in relation to an ongoing history of migration rather than a consequence of it.[1] It is important to note that postmigration does not necessarily designate the condition of a subject that lives with the direct effects of having migrated. Neither does it merely designate the condition of coming from a family with a migration experience. In contrast to these particularizing notions, my use of postmigration refers to a cultural conjuncture that reshapes and transforms the question of belonging at large. Being a migrant and living in a postmigration condition are as related to one another as being a non-migrant and living in a postmigration condition. Therefore, I do not use the term as a proper name such as 'postmigrant' to describe an individual or a group. That is to say, rather than denoting a subject, in this study, postmigration refers to the conditioning of positionalities in relation to changes in modes of cultural attachment, not only affecting "people who are [or have been] themselves directly 'on the move' but also the locales in which they settle, converting them to translocational spaces, thereby affecting in different ways all who live within these spaces" (Anthias 2008: 11). Similar to Homi Bhabha's description of the term postcolo-

---

1 The term postmigration is not a widely used concept in migration studies in Germany. It finds a rather different use in the field of psychology, where it is often opposed to pre-migration to describe particular behavioral, psychological, and attitudinal changes of migrants. In this sense, it is employed to observe the psychological impact of migration on individuals or groups and carries with it connotations of pathologization, summarized with terms like 'postmigration disorder' or 'postmigration trauma'. In my study, however, the term describes how migration changes the sociomaterial worlds it touches, be it directly or indirectly, including the worlds of those who seem to have not changed their place of living.

nial, here the prefix *post* points to the "shifting, strategically displaced time," bringing into play a history of migration alongside and within the present yet also "touching the future on its hither side," signposting the potential of emergence of future cultural politics of belonging and dynamics of attachment (Bhabha 1994: 18; 35). With this dimension of futurity, it also accentuates unpredictability. The label 'guest worker' embodies this conspicuously. Instead of returning to their departure country, as it was largely expected and narrated, many stayed and preferred to build a life in a place in which they have invested economically, bodily, affectively as well as intellectually, and artistically. The contemporary postmigration condition is a situation in which this kind of unforseeability of the effects of migration should be taken as constitutive of the ongoing and the not-yet present.

Furthermore, in this work, *Neuer Feminismus* indicates the emergence of particular forms of popfeminism in contemporary Germany. The term Neuer Feminismus has appeared in the media and scholarly texts since around 2006. The most comprehensive collection of essays written on Neuer Feminismus as a particular turn of feminism in Germany was collected in the November 2008 issue of *Feministische Studien*. As the editors of this collection remark in their introduction, although most authors of this issue assert that there is a need for a new kind of feminism, questions as to "what is to be understood under 'new' and what kind of feminism are we talking about" remain unanswered (Casale, Gerhard, and Wischerman 2008: 9). In this issue, Neuer Feminismus is characterized as media-oriented, transnational and as a demand posed by "women of the new generation" (ibid: 9). Transnationality stands here largely for an adaptation of a US-based popfeminism existing since the 1980s. However, with particular focus on Lady Bitch Ray, I claim, rather than just a belated copy of US popfeminism, Neuer Feminismus is responding to and emerging with a particular historical and discursive juncture in a postmigration condition. Though it certainly shows transnational inspirations (including the US), it is nevertheless crucial to take note of its production of culturally different feminist positionalities in Germany. In other words, Neuer Feminismus does not only come into being by means of transnational references, but is itself also a product of locationally specific processes of transculturation.

I am aware of the vagueness of the term and of its risk of inscribing a temporal linearity by means of an old/new binary. Crucially, however, my conceptualization of Neuer Feminismus suggests an abandonment of the rhetoric of generationalism.[2] That is because "the old ones do not always have to give way for the new [and] the new do not have to completely break with the old" (Halberstam 2012: 2). Feminists who apply a generationalism to the history of feminism, in Jack Halberstam's words, run the risk of being "more Freudian than Freud himself" since they get trapped in simplistic quasi-oedipal narratives involving a struggle for symbolic matricide; in this logic independence comes only with a radical rejection of one's mother's ideals (ibid: 3). As I discuss in chapter one, this logic is often applied to analyses of Neuer Feminismus. Since it relies on heteronormative relations and ideas of familial bonds at the basis of national homogeneity, it inevitably excludes queer (and) migrant feminist histories and present interventions. I content that, rather than a generational shift playing out in transmissions of and reactions to feminist sentiment in a continuous mother-daughter dynamic, the newness in Neuer Feminismus is a conceptual shift that comes about through a reconfiguration of feminist politics in relation to changes in Germany's cultural cartographies.

To move into a greater depth of field for analyses of popfeminism in Germany, I suggest supplementary narratives are needed to compliment the focus on sexual explicitness as the singular characteristic and

---

2   Therefore, in this work, I do not use terms such as 'first wave', 'second' or 'third wave' feminism, since these too heavily suggest a logic of generationalism. Neither do I use 'first', 'second' or 'third generation' to describe the (grand)children of migrants born and/or raised in Germany. By this, I do, however, not propose a tabooization of the term 'generation', since there are of course moments when its meaning remains ambiguous or when it can be employed as strategically straight-forward.

exclusive performative trademark. As I show in chapter one, the issue of sexual objectification of women in pop culture has dominated both sides, affirmative and critical, in the debate on what popfeminism fights for, or fails to fight against. This rhetoric tends to exclude those who do associate with feminism but do not affirm or see sexual explicitness as a core principal of emancipation. With this in mind, my study highlights transculturality as a conceptual supplement to thicken the description of Neuer Feminismus, and aims to position popfeminism in an intimate dialogue with decolonial critique so as to situate contemporary feminist practices in Germany in the current postmigration condition.

The term transculturation was coined in the 1940s by the Cuban anthropologist Fernando Ortiz to explain the asymmetric interdependency of cultures, or, more crudely, to explain how cultural interaction is way more complex than what the terms 'integration,' 'assimilation,' and 'acculturation' can tell us. According to Encarnación Gutiérrez Rodríguez, transculturation "raises the question of the colonial imperialist and economic links between Europe and other parts of the world by focusing on the impact of these histories on everyday culture" and by "tracing interdependencies between current processes of migration and European history" (Gutiérrez Rodríguez 2010a: 116). With this in mind, transculturation, in this study, figures as an essential concept referring to the relational entanglements between histories of migration and current forms of popfeminism in Germany.

For some critics, the issue of how gender and sexuality play out in pop culture, of whether there is potential subversiveness or a mere imposition of consumerist lifestyles also points to the political possibilities popfeminism has to offer—or, from another perspective, the lack thereof. Most often, popfeminism is seen as symptomatic of postfeminism, which is used as an umbrella label to criticize the backlash against feminism occurring in the late 1970s and 80s. This view portrays postfeminism as inherently postpolitical, as an ironic remainder or a commodified leftover after the death of feminism, or just a parody of feminist achievements. Accordingly, pop culture at large becomes the site in which this parody of feminism plays out most forcefully (McRobbie 2009; Faludi 1992; Modleski 1991). In her critique of postfeminism, Tania Modleski claims, for instance, that there is no need to look for the image of femininity *in* pop culture because pop culture as such already *represents* dominant ideas of femininity, with all its stereotypical characteristics of passivity and unbridled consumerism (Modleski 1991). Similarly, according to Yvonne Tasker and Diane Negra, "[p]ostfeminist culture's centralization of an affluent elite certainly entails an empathic individualism [and] elevates consumption as a strategy for healing those dissatisfactions that might alternatively be understood in terms of social ills and discontents" (Tasker/Negra 2007: 2). In Angela McRobbie's view, postfeminism becomes little else than a "daughter's revenge," that is, a depoliticized style-mania of 'spoiled' though witty 'girls' comfortable with the vacuous utopia of neoliberal consumerism and, in fact, complacently celebrating the achievements of Western feminism (McRobbie 2009: 40). Moreover, as McRobbie writes, the postfeminist shift signals a "re-colonising meachanism in contemporary popular culture" which "re-instates racial hierarchies within the field of femininity invoking, across the visual field, a norm of nostalgic whiteness" (ibid: 43). This is why Yvonne Tasker and Diane Negra call post/popfeminism "white and middle class by default" (Tasker/Negra 2007: 2).

For others, however, it is quite the opposite: postfeminism is "a product the interventions of women of color and lesbian theorists into the feminist debate, as it takes into account the demands of marginalized and colonized cultures for a non-ethnocentric and non-heterosexist feminism" (Genz/Brabon 2009: 121). As Ann Brook claims, postfeminism is not about "a depoliticization of feminism, but a political shift" expressing "the intersection of feminism with postmodernism, poststructuralism and post-colonialism, and as such represents a dynamic movement capable of challenging modernist, patriarchal and imperialist frameworks" (Brooks 2002: 4). Similarly refuting the perception of pop culture as the sphere of mere reinforcement of gender inequalities, bell hooks writes, pop cultural politics enables feminism to open itself to a "critical dialogue with the uneducated poor [and] the black underclass," since pop culture itself "may very well be 'the' central future location of resistance struggle, a meeting place where new and radical happenings can occur" (Hooks 1990: 31).

I believe that, especially in the contemporary network age, it is difficult, if not impossible to uphold either of the polarized views, as popfeminism is necessarily both, participating in a hegemonic and marginal discourse at once. Most crucially, it has to be noted that there is no such thing as one kind of popfeminism. There are varieties and differences in terms of politics and feminist positioning. The central question is therefore: who gets to define popfeminism? For the art and politics of interpretation are always-already imbricated with the object to be interpreted. In short, reading and analyzing popfeminism participates in its practice. Part of popfeminism's whiteness is created by white lenses of interpretation (and in some cases no less so by self-proclaimed critically white lenses). It matters what examples we choose and with what kind of discurses we entangle these examples in. Or put it differently: Who are those popfeminists? Is it Madonna or Lil' Kim? Lady Gaga or Nicki Minaj? Lily Allen or M.I.A? Charlotte Roche or Lady Bitch Ray? While all these figures can certainly be associated with established aesthetics of popfeminism, it is nevertheless crucial to place them in a greater analytic depth of field to see the different forms of popfeminism and the discursive fields of action they occupy. The issue hereby is not to point to marginalized ethnic identities as exceptions in their creation of differences, but to processes of how feminist positions emerge relationally, stretching distances and traversing differences between various popfeminist practitioners. In fact, as Kimberly Springer observes, "studies of postfeminism have studiously noted that many of its icons are white and cited the absence of women of color, but the analysis seems to stop there" (Springer 2007: 249). Hence, this study aims at not stopping short, but at expanding the meaning of current popfeminism in Germany, namely Neuer Feminismus, and at looking for the types of exclusion resulting from stopping short.

To make matters worse, one could even say that postfeminism is itself a thing of the past, as the term seems to be strangely outdated, as if it is stuck in the debate of whether the project of feminism as such is still alive. 'Postfeminism' seems out of sync with our queer times marked by "the withering away of old social models of desire, gender, and sexuality" and the emergence of "potent new forms of relation, intimacy, technology, and embodiment" (Halberstam 2012: 25). The relevant question raised by this situation is not whether feminism is dead or alive, but rather how feminist subjectivities can be diversely and transversely embodied and proliferated. Postfeminism as a label does not quite capture currently circulating forms of feminist politics that engage with gender, sexuality, and embodiment across multiplicities of "onto-epistemological" frameworks (Barad 2007). After all, "[f]eminist embodiment […] is not about […] a reified body, female or otherwise, but about nodes in fields, inflections in orientations, and responsibility of difference in material-semiotic fields of meaning" (Harraway 1997: 121). According to Rosi Braidotti, these transversal feminist subjectivities are animated by "a complex and articulate notion of 'embodiment'" inherent in a "living and lived body, as well as the idea of a transgenerational, nonlinear memory of one's belonging" (Braidotti 2013: 130). Rather than relying on distinct categories of difference and their intersections, the issue of producing a feminist subject concerns how "their interaction and their shifting relations emerge as more significant than any identity they may actually engender" (ibid: 129–130). What is at stake in analyzing these embodied categories is therefore not the difference between them, but the relational conditions that make the appearance of differences possible.

If postfeminism's social critique has worked with and brought forth notions of intersectionality, today's post-queer, transcultural, new materialist forms of feminist critique shift towards issues of entanglement and interference "to rethink race, sexuality, and gender as concatenations, unstable assemblages of revolving and devolving energies, rather than intersectional coordinates" (Puar 2007: 195). While it has been powerfully expanding the scope of feminist inquiry, intersectional thought is limited due to its analytical reliance on distinct, pre-existing social categories in the explanation of social privileges and disadvantages. Although the intersectional approach is definitely helpful to draw the outlines of complex positional maps, we need other approaches to give us further insight into the multi-dimensionality of these maps. This means, in order to make sense of how these positionalities come into being, we need more intricate "genealogies of the [...] contingent structural relations of power" (Barad 2001: 99).

Since positionalities and their corporealities are produced within multiply entangled webs of difference, categories that do not seem to play an immediate representational role should not be treated as external but seen as part of the dynamic multidimensional formation of what ends up to be framed as representation. "Identities are not separable, they do not intersect," Barad assures us; "rather identity formation must be understood in terms of the topological dynamics of iterative intra-activity" (ibid: 99). Employing Barad's model in her critical reflection on intersectional thought, Nina Lykke asserts that the idea of intersectionality has to be broadened to processes of *intra-action*. In contrast to interaction, which "is something that takes place between bounded entities, clashing against each other but not generating mutual transformations [...] intra-action refers to the interplay between nonbounded phenomena which interpenetrate and mutually transform each other while interplaying" (Lykke 2012: 208). Given that categories are always already relationally intertwined, primary analytic focus is not only to be laid on points of intersection, but also on the convoluted patterns of interplay.

In this respect, attention to complex relational conditions offers ways to map out not only linkages, but also those discursive dynamics that render certain positionalities unlinkable and, in fact, unthinkable because they are not (yet) intersecting. Those unrepresented and unrepresentable positionalities might be externalized because they are rhetorically avoided, taken ironically, or contradictorily, due to gaps, traps, and dead ends in the existing discourses. Therefore, as Evelien Geerts and Iris van der Tuin write, we need "an onto-epistemological understanding of the emergence of both hierarchical power relations and relations that are subversive because they cannot be understood along the lines of a restrictive power hierarchy" (Geerts/van der Tuin 2013: 177). For positionalities become mutually exclusive when the existing framework renders certain linkages ineffable.

Situating Lady Bitch Ray's feminist politics in the current popfeminist scene in Germany, in chapter one, I focus specifically on her toying with terms, concepts, and positions constructed as mutually exclusive. Analytically, I am less interested in extrapolating her 'intention' than in tracing the discursive contradictions emerging in her performance. In the first chapter, I argue that it is by means of these contradictions and ambivalences that she challenges the existing framework of feminism in postmigration Germany. In my attempt to make sense of these dynamics of contradiction, I explore the transcultural dimension formed in her performance by analyzing how she dis- and reentangles ethnically coded terms of 'emancipation', and poses questions as to who is entitled to represent 'emancipation'. Her performance opens up ways to discuss certain notions of emancipation bound up with 'Germanness' and discursively opposed to 'Turkishness'. Her way of dealing with the established categories of belonging displays how and under which conditions a feminist positionality is (not) 'properly' embodied. This is how her performance animates a diverse set of feminist conceptions of emancipation and moves through transcultural feminist geographies and their somatic signs. Her emphasis on her 'Turkishness' functions hereby as a form of self-marking which runs against discourses of 'integration' and 'assimilation'. With this in mind, in the first chapter, I conceptualize her markers of 'Turkishness' as manifesting a *deliberate failure of passing*.

In my analysis of her paradoxical mode of positioning, I draw on what Walter Mignolo has described as "epistemic disobedience" (Mignolo 2009). According to Mignolo, epistemic disobedience is a reworking of the concepts attached to Western modernity by "delinking" them from their Eurocentric, secular-modernist interpretations (Mignolo 2007). In my analysis, Lady Bitch Ray de-links 'emancipation' from Western feminist paternalism and recasts it ambiguously, enabling multiple possible meanings which are seemingly paradoxical in practice. She brings together different forms of feminism despite, or, because of the resulting rhetorical contradictions. In fact, her sexual explicitness thereby operates by no means as an unquestioned support of Western feminist notions of emancipation, or an outright plea for sexual promiscuity. Rather it creates rhetorical tensions and ambiguities, calling for practices of *conceptual promiscuity*.

A pioneering artist of what came to be called Neuer Feminismus, Lady Bitch Ray forms a popfeminism that engages openly with questions of transculturality. What makes her performance particularly powerful is the fact that her rhetoric evokes the black, migrant and queer feminist interventions of early 1990s usually written out of the history of German feminism. Gleaning concepts and perspectives from scholars and activists engaged in pushing feminism in Germany beyond ethnocentric understandings of gender politics, I see Lady Bitch Ray's feminism as a project of *translingualization*. A central aspect in this is her employment of the words 'bitch, 'hure', and 'oruspu', which, in her use, reappropriate forms of racialized, gendered, sexualized or otherwise injurious speech. Tracing the genealogies of otherization and reappropriation of these terms, chapter one shows how she activates a feminism that is transnational yet at the same time locationally specific.

Following Susan Stanford Friedman's theorization of locational feminism, in this study, I foreground the specificities of Germany's contemporary cultural landscape and the ways they are shaped through migration. "A locational approach to feminism," Friedman writes,

"incorporates diverse formations because its positional analysis requires a kind of geopolitical literacy built out of a recognition of how different times and places produce different and changing gender systems as these intersect with other different and changing societal stratifications and movements for social justice. Locational feminism thus encourages the study of difference in all its manifestations without being limited to it, without establishing impermeable borders that inhibit the production and visibility of ongoing intercultural exchange and hybridity." (1998: 5)

This view on locationality is therefore far away from the celebration of national borders and so-called 'local' subjects, distancing itself from the anxiety surrounding the terms locationality and local. These terms produce a sense of skepticism, if not suspicion, as they are often perceived to be redrawing borders and seal off particular environments from their outsides. On the contrary, in the postmigration era, a locational approach provides perspectives on how the translocal is always already present within the local. For a feminist position, then, the politics of location and locationality can be employed against sweeping generalizations of what feminism is supposed to be or supposed to have developed from. As Standford Friedman puts it, "feminism seldom arises in purely indigenous forms, but, like culture itself, develops syncretistically out of a transcultural interaction with others" (ibid: 5).

Feminism's constitutive transculturality and its interrelation to migration is emphasized by Donna Gabaccia, who writes in her *From the Other Side*: "American womanhood had changed significantly as immigrants became American women, so that the female American models confronting immigrant women today are far different from those of the past" (1994: xv). For Gabaccia, this view does not assume an asymmetrical 'successful' integration model of those women who immigrated to the US, but rather tries to express how 'immigrant women' have "repeatedly challenged the American notion of biological difference in both its 'racial' and its 'sexual' varieties" (ibid: xii). Thus, "as foreign woman crossed over from the other side, they did not simply adjust to American life—they redefined the meaning of American womanhood" (ibid: xxiii). In fact, transculturality is hereby not simply a result of two cultures meeting by means of migration. For migrants did not just carry homogenous ethnic identities into a new setting, but brought also with them diverse "female traditions found within their native cultures" (ibid:, xi). In a postmigration condition, then, the emergence of new positionalities is a result of multiply converging histories (including various forms of feminism). In her *Cartographies of Diaspora*, Avtar Brah writes with respect to the experience of Asian and black female migrants and their children in the UK: because of its creation of new positionalities, migration has "challenge[d] the idea of [a] continuous, uninterrupted" Britishness (1996: 195). In this sense, a transcultural locational perspective focuses on migrants and their non-migrant children as agents within processes of transculturation, bringing about re-appraisals of what counts as 'local'.

Especially since the late 1950s and early 1970s, when the first wave of migrant workers and intellectuals arrived, they became not only a substantial part of the German economy, but also transformed the meaning of Germanness.[3] The resulting positional entanglements urge us "to rethink our understanding of contemporary West German culture and feminist models of minority discourse" (Adelson 1993: 128). From a transcultural locational feminist perspective, then, "[a] rigorous discussion of feminist positionalities—and of the function of positionality in contemporary feminist discourse—reveals historicized and racialized constructions of gender as well as engendered and racialized construction of German history and national identity" (ibid: 127). And the politics of Neuer Feminismus, particularly (but not exclusively) Lady Bitch Ray's, display the emergence of these kinds of transcultural locational feminist entanglements. In fact, Lady Bitch Ray's toying with the word 'Kanackin' vividly animates these entanglements by intertwining specific colonial histories, postwar migration experiences, strategically essentialist migrant, and queer feminist interventions in Germany. Through this kind of diffraction, it sheds light on the enmeshed and messy trajectory of feminism in Germany, signaling what Susan Stanford Friedman refers to as feminist politics "beyond gender" (Stanford Friedman 1998: 18). According to Friedman, "moving beyond gender does not mean forgetting it, but rather returning to it a newly

---

3 For a comprehensive cultural analysis of this, see Gutiérrez Rodríguez 1999; for a literary analysis, see Adelson 2005; and for a detailed historical overview, see: Chin 2007.

spatialized way," that is, a locationally-specic way (ibid: 18). Focusing on the links between the Anglo-American and the German feminist debate, Gudrun-Axeli Knapp has refererred to this locational return as a form of "reclaiming baggage" which she describes as

"a time-consuming activity, resembling the psychoanalytical process of '*Erinnern, Wiederholen, Durcharbeiten*'. In the field of theory it works by remembering, by historicizing, contextualizing and comparing with respect to both levels: the so-called ontological level dealing with questions of 'what is' and the epistemological level of how we look at it. And, in a self-reflexive move, it would take up the question of how both of these levels are interrelated in contemporary culture and society and how they shape one's own conditions of proposing." (2005: 260)

With this in mind, in this study I claim that it is not enough to focus on sexual explicitness in analyses of popfeminism. For the contemporary postmigration condition requires a focus on the transcultural entanglements produced by current popfeminist politics in Germany.

As I show in chapter three, in the group discussions I conducted with Turkish-German university students, forms of positioning emerged that delinked or cut across binary discourses and thereby marked a potential for more expansive understandings of what feminism is or ought to be. In my interpretation of the participants' interpretation of Lady Bitch Ray's music video, this potential materialized in the gaps of discourses, being animated more with the unsaid than with the said. Analyzing the participants' shifting attachments, their critical, I conceptualize the points of the discussion at which participants shifted in between negating and affirming Lady Bitch Ray's feminism as *aposiopetic positioning*. It describes the moments when the discussion is detoured, paused, or became silent, and when the available language was not trusted because it would place the speaker into reductionist positional molds. This sense of insufficiency of the available discourse became particularly evident in one participant's use of aposiopesis, a figure of speech which leaves the sentence unfinished and creates a present absence: "I love feminists, but if this is feminism…" This aposiopetic phrase is a variant of "I'm not a feminist but…," which is a form of positioning that marks an ambiguous rhetorical sliding along the boundaries of a feminist standpoint (Griffin 1989). Rather than just rejecting feminism wholesale, it can create the potential to make a feminist statement without cornering oneself in the assumed dogmas and orthodoxies associated with the history of feminism. According to Beverly Skeggs, the phrase 'I'm not a feminist but…' "may display a refusal to be fixed into place as a feminist" or indicate "the inability to position oneself as feminist because of confusing and contradictory messages about what feminism really is" (Skeggs 1997: 142). As I discuss in the third and last chapter of this study, as a Turkish-German living in Germany, Selin (a participant) avoids the language that would trap her into a cliché image of 'Turkishness', namely being insistent on traditions incompatible with feminism.

As for my use of language, I am very well aware of the hazardous moves involved in using distinct markers of belonging in an empirical analysis. After having introduced the major themes of my dissertation at conferences and other academic and non-academic occasions, I often encounter the same question, a question that points to the complexity of the cultural politics of belonging in postmigration Germany: why do I insist on Lady Bitch Ray's Turkishness? Referring to the controversy and confusion around her performance (in the media and among feminist critics), in chapter one, I aim to address this question by asking: why does Lady Bitch Ray insist on her Turkishness?

In fact, the mere occurrence of the term 'Turkishness' in my analysis is often perceived as an essentializing gesture on my part. Though the use of such categories might be risky, I am nevertheless convinced that avoiding them is not always less risky, as this does not automatically guarantee a non-essentialist position. And using these loaded terms does not always mean that one unquestionably reproduces the categories at hand. In this respect, I treat these categories as "external attractors, stimulants or points of reference" (Braidotti 2013: 40). Rather than blacklisting certain terms, by analyzing and interpreting the group discussions, I present how, in a situated empirical setting, these categories come into being and are already under erasure, awkwardly supplementing one another and themselves.

Although contemporary cultural imaginaries in Europe deal with de-binarizations of ethno-cultural belonging in relation to migration (whether this is seen as a blessing or a curse), this condition does not necessarily bring about a disappearance of ethnicized vocabulary. The production of 'Turkishness' in Germany is a good example for this. After all, 'Turkishness' in Germany is intertwined with locationally specific histories and experiences of cultural difference. This is why a person born and raised in Germany but identifying herself as a 'Turk' or 'Kurd' (or whatever else) should not necessarily be perceived as radically renouncing 'Germanness', but as articulating a kind of 'Turkishness' or 'Kurdishness' that cannot be understood without its entanglement with 'Germanness' and other forms of ethnic marking in Germany.

These kinds of entanglements were acted out, directly and indirectly, in the group discussions I conducted. The participants dislocated and dispersed cultural markers, moving them from one locale to another, dynamically situating them in transcultural geographies that traverse nation-state borders. Their use of these markers does not necessarily entail an attachment to a specific geographic place but signifies forms of nomadic belonging that problematizes the rhetorical recourse to an originary territory. Therefore, I use Floya Anthias' conceptualization of "translocational positionality" to map out the participants' *territorial* movement. Anthias' theorization effectively captures the relation between the construction of identity and its locations. As she writes, "translocational positionality addresses issues of identity in terms of locations which are not fixed but are context, meaning and time related and which therefore involve shifts and contradictions" (Anthias 2008, 5). Accordingly, "the focus on location (and translocation)" is crucial, since it "recognises the importance of context, the situated nature of claims and attributions and their production in complex and shifting locales" (Anthias 2002: 502).

The forms of attachment articulated by the participants by means of cultural markers can be compared to Avtar Brah's notion of "diasporic space," a space within which "multiple subject positions are juxtaposed, contested, proclaimed or disavowed" (Brah 1996: 208). This diasporic space is formed through "psychic investment in emotionally charged bonds with family and relations" (ibid: 43). As Brah argues, these relations come into being and are upheld through affective negotiation, and tend to get articulated in language through phrases like "not letting family down" (ibid: 78). In fact, in their debate on Lady Bitch Ray's performance, the participants circled around issues related to familial bonds. The phrase that stuck out in one of the group discussions was *looking one's parents in the eyes*, which hints at the affective links through which certain norms and values are negotiated and contested.

Drawing on Sara Ahmed's reading of politics involved in the exchange and circulation of emotion, I further show that, rather than prescriptive, these norms and values are movable referents within a system of empathy. According to Ahmed, "emotions should not be regarded as psychological states but as social and cultural practices" (Ahmed 2004: 9). Analyzing feelings, she writes, can give us insight into how emotions take on a "form of cultural politics or world making," which is always bound to an investment in "particular structures" (ibid: 12). With this in mind, I present how the participants constructed the family as an *affectively contested testing-ground*, a site in which ideals of morality and their practices are assessed via politics of emotion. It is a site in which what is right and what is wrong is becoming defined.

Moreover, I show how the discussants moved between distancing themselves from Lady Bitch Ray's politics and finding points of identification. This became apparent in their switching between personal pronouns. They moved back and forth between referring to the German-Turkish youth as *they* and *we*. In their search for a way to understand Lady Bitch Ray's performance, being born and raised in Germany was, at times, seen as the reason for her excessive use of sexual explicitness (and implied desires for 'assimilation'). However, the question was also to what extent they could uphold such a view, since they themselves were also born and raised in Germany. This conceptual confrontation became particularly apparent in the exchange between two participants. Their conversation shifted from an argumentative distance—from talking *about* Lady Bitch Ray, marked by the pronoun *she*—to the direct dialogical proximity of the *I* and *You*, when one participant confronted the other: "I am also born and raised here. What are you trying to say?" In my interpretation, this moment encapsulates the participants' ambiguous rhetorical construction of 'Germanness', which is turned into what Yoko Tawada, a German-Japanese poet, has called *the second person I*. Rather than being secondary and therewith distanced, 'Germanness', I argue here becomes an at once intimate and detached positionality.

Chapter 3 ends with the participants' conception of Lady Bitch Ray's feminism. I explore the participants' rhetorical moves in their search for answers to the question of what Lady Bitch Ray's politics is about, for, and against. In this part, I argue that the participants' paradoxically positioned answers to this question outlined a potential for a not-yet-existing transcultural feminist discourse. This potential emerged from the contradictory entanglements and the gaps and traps occurring in the search for position vis-à-vis Lady Bitch Ray's politics and feminism at large.

In dealing with discursive absences, methodologically, this study engages in a form of "deliberate unlearning" (Savage 2011: 81). It works with empirical data at hand in a way that it seeks to problematize the readily available analytic vocabulary. Deliberate unlearning, as David Beer writes in *Punk Sociology*, is about re-opening, questioning, and rearranging "our established ways of working and [...] our established ideas and concepts" and "see[ing] potentially new or mutated ways of doing sociology and being sociologists" (Beer 2014: 41). With this in mind, my aim is, on the one hand, to situate and ground my own perspective, and, on the other, give the material enough room to move and make me move beyond my perspective. For that, one needs to take on the risks of revisiting, questioning, and unlearning the concepts, terms, and understandings that one takes for granted. A guiding motto of this study is therefore borrowed from a statement written on an artwork by Jimmie Durham: "I forgot what I was going to say." My approach aims to be open to experimentation and improvisation—not as off-the-cuff inventiveness, but in the sense of letting the process interfere with the limitations of the initial framework. This approach is of particular value in the sociological field of identity politics and migration, because the methodological frameworks of sociology tend to reinscribe binaries between the West and its others. In fact, the very language of analysis is shaped by "the social norms, structures, and values characterizing the so-called Western societies as a universal parameter for defining what modern societies are" and what its empirical subjects represent (Gutiérrez Rodríguez /Boatcă/Costa 2010: 1). European migration studies, as Encarnación Gutiérrez Rodríguez has pointed out, often presents itself "in a managerial language, embedded in methodological nationalism, classifying and quantifying migrants and post/migrants and targeting these groups as objects of governance" (Gutiérrez Rodríguez 2010d: 30). "[T]ranscultural translation" bears a methodological potential to question this hegemonic discourse, since it foregrounds the productive exchanges and the interplay between empirical data and the language available to represent them (ibid: 17-36). Since my research is situated in a trilingual framework—German, Turkish and English—the issue of translation takes on a particularly prominent role. In my interpretations, I aim to deal productively with the existing layers of unstranslatability in order to engage with the participants' critical and creative use of the available linguistic repertoire.

In quantitative terms, three group discussions could be considered as not 'enough'. However, reviewing these three discussions, I realized that they provided more than enough material for a productive empirical study. In fact, my sense of saturation with regard to the collected data is formed by a politico-methodological understanding, which stands against the over-accumulation of data on the basis of an assumption that sheer quantity brings about a greater quality and the selection of a specific set with rigid lines drawn between productive and unproductive, consumable and not consumable data. Instead of this quantity paradigm, there is the possibility of efficiently using of the data at hand (and their always-already-existing density and thickness), by not simply discarding parts of the data and turning them into "wasted knowledges" (de Sousa Santos 2004). Indeed, I sensed that a further collection of data would have inevitably led to a de-privileging of the purportedly unproductive moments within the already collected set. From this emerged my decision to treat those moments in which the group discussion participants contradicted themselves, went off topic, or remained awkwardly silent, as primary points of analysis.

Grounded Theory is, in this respect, allows the researcher to work closely with the empirical material through processes of coding: initial coding, selective coding and theoretical coding (discussed in chapter two). These coding processes provide ways to create thick categories with a relatively low amount of collected material. However, Grounded Theory is also limited by its orientation towards *what is said* and, therefore, what is directly represented in the data. In order to methodologically engage with the gaps and silences and to ground what remained unsaid, I use *Situational Analysis*. Developed by Adele Clarke, Situational Analysis combines the basic principles of Grounded Theory with a deconstructionist methodology. In chapter two, I elaborate on how Situational Analysis' use of maps makes it possible to pay attention to absences and emergences. The chapter closes with a presentation of the maps that emerged from the data gathered in the group discussions.

It is crucial to note that it was not merely my political predisposition and initial choices in terms of research strategies, but primarily the data themselves—with all their absences and inconsistencies, and the resulting moments of reconsideration, consternation—that pushed this study towards a decolonizing approach to methodology. After all, decolonizing means to scrutinize the representational force of the available discourses and work for possibilities of "alternative ways of knowing," interpreting, representing (Tuhiwai Smith 2007: 166). To sense alternative ways of understanding and participate in their potential emergence, this study seeks to be attentive to the categories and social worlds that did not make it into language, or did not pass from one language into another—attentive to the entangled constructions of presence and absence, to what is there, what is not there, and what is within the knot, knit into the 'not'.

„Ich bin 'ne Kanackin"
Decolonizing Pop Feminism

> It is not that I am against feminism: I'm appalled at what it became. Originally, there was nothing wrong with my seeing myself as a feminist; I thought it was adding to how we were going to understand this world.
>
> SYLVIA WYNTER/PROUD FLESH

What was initiated by a handful of young artists and authors in the mid-2000s became seen as a feminist renaissance, a paradigmatic shift towards "Playing Dirty," as the title of Stephanie Kirchner's 2008 Time Magazine article reads. Featuring an image of Lady Bitch Ray, captioned "Embracing Scandal," and listing works such as Wir Alpha-Mädchen (We Alphagirls) and Neue Deutsche Mädchen (New German Girls), Kirchner's article announces the rise of popfeminism in Germany. According to Kirchner (2008), these fairly recent popcultural interventions launch a new form of feminist aesthetics characterized primarily by "explicit language, personal tone and sometimes infantile humor" As Kirchner concludes, this use of explicit language is not "entirely new" but signals a delayed arrival of the popfeminism that emerged in the US more than two decades ago.

Towards the end of her article, Kirchner poses an interesting question: why has Germany been lagging behind in practicing popfeminism? However tempting it is, especially concerning the no doubt existing similarities between the popfeminisms in the US and Germany, this question is nevertheless misleading, since it assumes feminism to be an abstract, universally defined phenomenon, as if it has one global story to tell and a single history to follow. Moreover, maintaining historical linearity, the logic of the question suggests that, since all problems feminism deals with are the same, so are the solutions. With this in mind, the universalist fallacy of this question produces a productive entry into a discussion on how the politics of location and difference play out in contemporary feminist theory and activism.

Popfeminism did not arrive late to Germany. Instead, as I claim in this chapter, what is called Neuer Feminismus is formed and re-modified within a particular historical and discursive juncture. That is to say, the rhetorical strategies that dominate the scene of Neuer Feminismus should be read as a "local configuration" shaped by "situated feminist experiences" (Ferree 2012: 16). As I note in the introduction, this does not entail disregard towards the global, transnational dynamics occurring across different locations. Convinced that it is crucial to overcome the fear of 'going local', I argue that rather than being a mere adaptation, Germany's Neuer Feminismus has its own chronotopic frame: it entangles transnational feminisms in a context where space and time is marked by the "peculiarity of German[y's] history" (Canning 2006: 164). In this respect, I argue, sexual explicitness as the sole analytic focus obscures the local peculiarities of popfeminism in Germany. To re-adjust and expand the analytic focus on Neuer Feminismus, I propose transculturality as a conceptual supplement. Looked at through this lens, the issue is not just that sexually explicit rhetoric became a dominant mode of expression in Neuer Feminismus, but how sexual explicitness materializes in relation to the transformative experiences shaped in Germany's postmigration condition. Considering Lady Bitch Ray as a pioneering artist of Neuer Feminismus, in the following part, I employ a transcultural approach to discuss what is new in Germany's new feminism.

BEYOND SEXUAL EXPLICITNESS—RESISTANCE THROUGH INSISTENCE

Lady Bitch Ray's appearance (beginning in 2006) and the publication of numerous literary works such as Charlotte Roche's Feuchtgebiete (2007), Sonja Eismann's Hot Topic (2007), Meredith Haaf et. al's Alpha-Mädchen (2008), Jana Hensel and Elisabeth Raether's Neue Deutsche Mädchen (2008), Sonia Rossi Fucking Berlin (2008) kicked off a popcultural turn in feminist rhetoric. As many scholars have noted, next to their combative tone and manifesto-like declarations, the most evident aspect that unites these projects is the emphasis on sexually explicit language (Herzing et al. 2013; Scharff 2013; Gill/Scharff 2013; Peglow/Engelmann 2013; Stehle 2012a; Villa et al. 2012; Spiers 2012; Volkmann 2011; Kauer 2009; Villa 2009). Whether with a sense of praise or with a critical tone, scholarly theorizations tend to define Neuer Feminismus with an already existing set of vocabulary, through which it threatens to become a one-to-one discursive equivalent of Anglo-American popfeminism (cf. Kauer 2009; Villa et al. 2012; Gill/Scharff 2013; Herzing et al. 2013). In such reading, sexual explicitness seems to operate as the prime determinant, often portrayed as an aesthetic end in itself. I do by no means claim that sexual explicitness should be disregarded in analyses of Neuer Feminismus. Instead, I suggest that, however central sexual explicitness is in the aesthetics of these works, focusing on it exclusively limits one's analytic scope. Reading Neuer Feminismus primarily as a struggle to assert raunchy rhetoric risks positing that sexual explicitness determines what popfeminism is all about; all there is to fight for.

To avoid this sense of an emancipatory panacea, sexual explicitness should rather be seen as a point of discursive departure. While it certainly reveals transnational feminist links, it also finds in Neuer Feminismus a new strategic, locationally specific use. A focus on transculturality can shed light on this. For instance, though Charlotte Roche is the most frequently named author associated with Neuer Feminismus, little else has been discussed than her penchant for punk-style raunchiness. Although it is known that she was born in Britain and raised by British parents in Germany, the implication of her culturally diverse background in her popfeminism has been largely overlooked.[1] An even more striking example is Sonia Rossi, whose book *Fucking Berlin* became, like Roche's Feuchtgebiete, a bestseller in 2008, reaching its eighteenth edition in 2011. In *Fucking Berlin*, Rossi recounts not only her life as a young woman who took on a side job as a sex worker but also her experiences as an Italian international student in Germany. Perhaps more implicitly, the authors of *Alpha Mädchen* and *Neue Deutsche Mädchen* bring together different experiences in East and West Germany.[2] These two books testify to the transcultural dynamics set in motion in the period "when the two women's movements collided in the process of Germany unification, each with its own vision of making a new, more feminist state" (Ferree 2012: 143). In all these works, sexual explicitness serves as a rhetorical strategy. It is, however, crucial to note the processes of transculturality in which it is shaped.

This transcultural dimension becomes most explicit in LBR's performance. Curiously, she is often omitted in analyses of popfeminism in Germany, as scholars tend to define Neuer Feminismus by foregrounding works of literature, taking *Feuchtgebiete*, *Alpha Mädchen* and *Neue Deutsche Mädchen* as prime examples (cf. Eismann 2007;

---

1   As she states in an interview: "Ich bin ganz Engländerin" (Roche 2011).
2   For instance, Jana Hensel, a co-author of *Neue Deutsche Mädchen* is also the author of *Zonenkinder*, a bestseller memoir about growing up in the GDR (2002). The book *Wir Alphamädchen* thematizes differences between Eastern and Western feminist movements and their respective achievements.

Volkmann 2011; Spiers 2012; Peglow/Engelmann 2013; Scharff 2013; Gill/Scharff 2013). If LBR is included in the analysis, her (trans)cultural background is either not mentioned at all, or it is considered as a secondary, almost coincidental element in her performance (cf. Kauer 2009; Villa 2009; Villa et al. 2012). Maria Stehle's article "Pop, Porn, and Rebellious Speech" is an exception in this respect. As Stehle writes, "LBR's political and theoretically informed interventions took place on two main sites, the music, and more specifically, the rap music scene, and, related to that, the mainstream German construction of 'German' and 'Turkish' identities" (Stehle 2011: 241). Examining Elfriede Jelinek, Charlotte Roche, and LBR as examples of a pornographic turn in Germany's feminism, Stehle argues that "for all three artists, sexually explicit language and imagery works in a particular context as rebellious speech" (Stehle 2011: 230).

Stehle's analysis is crucial for understanding the politics of cultural difference in Germany's popfeminism. However, it is worth pausing over the particularities of LBR's rebellious speech. As I claim, the rebelliousness of LBR's performance is not a result of her sexually explicit language per se. This means, if one reads her performance only as a manifestation of sexually explicit language, it does indeed not evince anything entirely new (to reuse Stephanie Kircher's phrase). In fact, a particular aspect of LBR's performance is the seemingly paradoxical mode of representation she crafts. Because she appears to be a perfectly 'Westernized' woman, her emphasis on her 'Turkishness' is perceived as contradictory. Echoing the media's sense of confusion in reaction to this seeming contradiction, Stehle asks, "why does she insist on being Turkish?" According to Stehle, it is LBR's "intention" to make us ask this question, to stir this kind of "confusion" (Stehle 2012: 160).

And this confusion is not just limited to the media. Many times, at conferences and at other academic occasions, I have been asked why I insist on LBR's Turkishness, or, in other words, why I 'turkify' her. The assimilationist logic behind this very question remains, however, often unnoticed. Assuming, or, ironically speaking, insisting LBR to be not 'Turkish' (despite her own claims), or, similarly, 'only' 'German' inadvertently confirms ethnically coded definitions of emancipation.

Image 2: Lady Bitch Ray in a talk show

Resource: still image from a talk show program

For what makes her not 'Turkish,' in this respect, is her sexually explicit rhetoric and imagery. The central paradox her performance raises is therefore: while seemingly having found a way around the gendered ethnic stereotype (i.e. the 'sexually suppressed Turkish woman'), she nevertheless resorts to marking herself as 'Turkish'. Precisely speaking, in her performance, sexually explicit rhetoric becomes rebellious in relation to her self-marking as 'Turkish', because it unsettles the essentializing paradigm of how gendered ethnic cliches are constructed in Germany.

The symbols and expressions that position her as 'Turkish' delink sexual explicitness from the dominant Western discourse of emancipation. Without her strategic self-ethnicization, as it was also revealed in my group discussions, the dimension of cultural difference would remain indiscernible, and cut short the provocative edge of her performance.

Yet, again, in her self-ethnicization, or self-turkification, she does by no means disassociate herself from 'Germanness'.[3] She subverts conventional notions of hybridity by claiming to be "a hundred percent Turkish and a hundred percent German" (Lady Bitch Ray 2012a). She thereby resists against the coercive "choice between heroic purity and decadent hybridity" (Gilroy 2010: 151). Put differently, she disrupts the normative algebra of hybridity, according to which the parts (usually thought to be two) inevitably total up to a whole, regardless of the number of fragments included: a little bit from here and a little bit from there.[4] Going beyond this reductionism, her statement claims the right to fully belong to both cultures at the same time, including all their internal differences and contradictions. Therefore, her self-marking as 'Turkish' neither signifies a radical withdrawal from 'Germanness' nor a well-defined culturally homogenous 'Turkishness'. And she further complicates her positionality by referring to herself as 'Kurdish' and emphasizing her Alevi-Muslim upbringing (Lady Bitch Ray 2012b: 14; 2014). Through this, she comments on how internal diversities and contradictions are swallowed up and suppressed with the conventional use of the term 'Turkishness'. Like Anzaldúa's "act of kneading," her self-marking involves a process of joining supposedly incompatible parts, enfolding them into a paradoxical whole (Anzaldúa 1987:81).

In fact, one could argue that the absence of ethno-cultural references would refashion her representation as a performance of passing. This means, part of the confusion and irritation she provokes comes

---

3   Here I borrow the term self-ethnicization from Sedef Gümen (1996). Furthermore, my use of 'self-turkification' draws on Encarnación Gutiérrez Rodríguez's conceptualization of "turkification" (1999).

4   This is, for instance, articulated in an early study on cultural hybridity in Germany entitled "Turkish-Germans, German-Turks or 'a little bit from here and a little from there'" [Türkische Deutsche, Deutsch Türken oder 'ein bißchen von da und ein bißchen von da'] (Hansen 1989).

with her unexpected denial of the all-too apparent opportunity of passing as 'German'.

Image 3: Identity card of artist Sinan Akkus

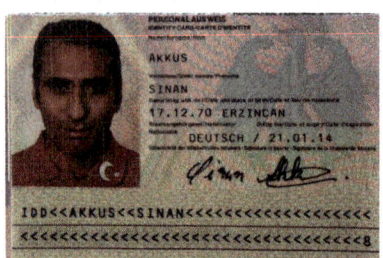

Resource: a still image from a documentary

This kind of deliberate failure of passing is powerfully visualized in Sinan Akkus' intervention in his German identity card (Image 3). Wearing a red shirt with the symbols of the Turkish flag (a half moon and a star), Akkus sidesteps clear-cut ethno-national identification. LBR's stitching of a half moon with a star on a red heart attached to her dress (Image 2) can be read in a similar fashion. In both cases, the visual emphasis on cultural difference deflects the possibility of passing. As a Turkish-German woman who speaks accent free German, who is 'well educated' and supposedly (sexually) 'emancipated', she "would," as Elger wrote for Spiegel, "be a perfect example for successful integration [...] one of those model-Turks" (Elger 2008). Indeed, she would be a suitable candidate for the BAMBI integration prize, which, since its introduction in 2010, has been given to soccer player Mesut Özil, rapper Bushido, and rabbi Daniel Alter. It is crucial to note that all prizewinners were born and raised in Germany. Ironically, the media controversy that followed Bushido's award centered only around his homophobic, misogynist and crime-glorifying lyrics—that is whether or not he deserves the award despite his 'problematic' public image—leaving out entirely the question of how a German-speaking -born and - raised person can win an 'integration' award in the first place.

In this respect, Lady Bitch Ray's refusal to pass as 'German' can be read as an answer to this question, and thus as a direct critique of the blurry line between the concepts of exclusion and inclusion. That is to say, it protests the kind of inclusionary gesture that resorts to a discourse of exclusion, seen in the BAMBI integration award. [5] Her self-positioning as 'Turkish' disrupts the very possibility of considering her as 'well integrated', a status and social standing which appears in popular idiom often in the guise of the 'eine(r) von uns' (one of us) rhetoric.

Image 4: 'Mesut Özil on the cover of the Deutsche Bahn magazine.[6]

Resource: still image

---

5 This mode of refusing to pass recalls Iola Leroy, the protagonist of Francis E.W. Harper's 1892 eponymous novel: "[b]y refusing to pass as white, Iola does more than assert her black identity; she also signals a specifically female form of social activism by subverting traditional gender roles" (Borgstrom 2006: 771).

6 It is important to note that every member of German national soccer team featured on the cover of this magazine. However, in terms of ethnocultural background, the team is very diverse, which creates a valid context for our discussion.

Rendering herself ineligible for being categorized as 'eine von uns', in a comment on the BAMBI integration award, she declares, "[i]f Bushido is integration, I am masturbation" (Lady Bitch Ray 2012a). This statement perfectly encapsulates her redeployment of sexual explicitness in the context of migration, and highlights the difference between her performance and the most commonly canonized works of Neuer Feminismus. In Roche's *Feuchgebiete*, too, masturbation is writ large. LBR, however, comes with a difference.

In this sense, her moaning (and other transgressive expressions of sexual pleasure) draws attention to a silenced span in the history of Germany's feminisms. That is to say, her emphasis on cultural difference signposts a largely submerged and unacknowledged feminist struggle in the 1990s, which I explore in the following part.

FEMINISM'S (M)OTHERS

In her article "The New German Feminisms: Of Wetlands and Alpha-Girls," Christina Scharff notes that the most vociferous moment of what is called 'German' feminism was historically situated in 1970s and 80s, and reawakened since 2006. Citing Ute Gerhard's *Atempause*, Scharff notes that the years in between "were constituted by a quieter period for feminist activism" (Scharff 2013: 265). In Gerhard's *Atempause*, this 'quiet period' is described as a result of a generational clash, or more specifically, a mother-daughter conflict. Accordingly, in order to develop their own "identity" and a gratifying sense of "self-esteem," in the 1990s, 'daughters of feminists' inevitably needed to distance themselves from their mothers' political goals and rhetorical conventions. Therefore they claimed that they "don't need feminism anymore," because they perceived it as an "antiquated" project (Gerhard 1999: 192).

Leaving aside the Freudian logic driving this argument, it is important to underline its risk of reinscribing a linear national narrative. Assuming that Germany's feminism is an inherited phenomenon occludes political potentials taking shape outside familial bonds. The question therefore is: what about those feminist activists whose mothers have not been considered as 'feminists' and were, in fact, subject to a suspicious Western feminist gaze, examined, even pitied for their supposed existence in deep oppression rooted in culturally determined patriarchic norms and traditions? As Myra Marx Ferree notes, it is the Western German feminist discourse of the 1970s and 80s that participated in and reproduced the representation of "non-German-origin women" as "backward, isolated and needy" and shored up "ethnic German women's own self-conception as benevolent mothers" in contradistinction to culturally different womanhood (Ferree 2012: 100-101). The discursive formation of 'German' feminism in the 1970s and 80s therefore has to be placed in relation with a contemporaneous construction of a 'non-German', 'not-yet-emancipated' woman.

Ambiguously, this dynamic contributed, on the one hand, to the supposed silence of feminism, but, on the other hand, it engendered other forms of feminism in the 1990s. That is to say, the very enactment of the supposed divide between Western gender equality and non-Western gender asymmetry was partly responsible for the fact that a certain status of 'emancipation' was taken for granted by the subsequent generation. In this sense, one could surmise that, if there is anything transmitted to the 'daughters' of 'German' feminists, it might be this sense of being advanced in the process of emancipation. Tellingly, lamenting the complacency of "the daughters of emancipation," Alice Schwarzer has nevertheless celebrated the election of Angela Merkel as German chancellor with the exclamation "Wir sind Kanzlerin" (We are Chancellor) (2005). Schwarzer's proclamation of victory for German womanhood at large reads like a reflection on a feminist triumph. This makes one wonder whether the narrative of feminism as an 'antiquated' project partly derives from those who complain the most about it.

Granted, the 'daughters' of 'German' feminists might have really been quieter in the 1990s. This does not mean, however, that there was no other feminist noise at all. The narrative of generational linearity represented in Gerhard's formulation omits queer interventions and migrant and diaspora feminist activism. Indeed, in the early 1990s, migrant women created their own feminist organizations, and a few years later, around 1995, Germany experienced a queering of feminism, known as the 'Butler boom' (cf. Gutiérrez Rodríguez 2010; Ferree 2012). Particularly notable events were, for instance, the founding of FeMigra (Feministische Migrantinnen Frankfurt) in 1991, a platform gathering migrant, black, diasporic, exilic feminists, and the migrant women congresses that took place in Bonn in 1994 and in Cologne in 1997. This means the feminist scene of 1990s was marked especially by a politicization of difference between and among women. The focus on ethnicity and class as intersectional dimensions and the erosion of gender as a stable category pushed feminism in Germany to make the leap beyond gender. Inspired by transnational movements such as Black, Chicana, Mestiza, queer and postcolonial feminism, migrant queer feminists were involved in attempts to shift activist rhetoric away from ethnocentric and heteronormative frameworks.[7] These intellectual, activist, and artistic contributions of this period tend to be left out in histories of feminism in Germany.

Paying attention to this feminist 'gap' helps to make sense of the ambiguous dynamics playing out in today's Neuer Feminismus. This becomes, for instance, rather obvious in Alice Schwarzer's relation to Charlotte Roche and LBR. Although she opposes the sexual explicitness and sex positive approach embodied by both artists, Schwarzer nevertheless engages in close dialogue with Roche while largely ignoring LBR. One senses a certain presence of the theme of generational continuity here, especially considering that Schwarzer hosted

---

7   For some of the early pioneering works in this debate, see: Kalpaka/Rätzel 1985; Oguntoye/Ayim 1986, Ayim 1993; Apostolidou 1994; Steyerl 1994; Gümen 1994, 1996; Derin 1996; Otyakmaz 1995; Gutiérrez Rodríguez 1996, 1999; Gelbin/Konuk/Piesche 1999; Yildiz 1999; Engel 1999.

Roche together with her mother Liz Busch for an interview about feminist mother-daughter dynamics (Roche and Busch 2001). Having an "overfeminist," EMMA-reading mother, it is as if Roche qualifies by default as a 'daughter of emancipation' (Dorn 2006: 140). Surprisingly, however, Schwarzer refused publishing an article by LBR in EMMA and declined writing the foreword to LBR's book *Bitchsm* (Lady Bitch Ray 2012b: 17, 452). One might speculate whether this is because LBR is not a 'daughter of emancipation', since, as an immigrant woman, her mother is, historically and discursively, positioned as 'not-yet-emancipated.'

Sticking with the mother-daughter formula for an instant, the ignorance towards LBR therefore also reflects the silenced history of her mother's feminism, so to speak. It is the omission of a history of other(s') feminisms in Germany that makes LBR's performance appear to be insignificant, rhetorically simplistic or just confusing.

Image 6: Alice Schwarzer with Charlotte Roche and Liz Busch.

Resource: www.emma.com

KANACK_IN—PLURALIZATIONS AND QUEERINGS

LBR's evocation of a polyvocal feminism resonates most forcefully in her statement "Ich bin eine Kanackin." Her self-identification as a 'female kanack' entwines a variegated set of political strategies, which are animated by her problematization of the conventions concerning positionings such as being 'Turkish', 'German,' or 'feminist'. Her performance draws on a local idiom, borrowing from German migrant feminists and West German feminist rhetoric while bringing in translocal aesthetics from mestiza, Chicana, US black, and African feminism. Her performance thus embodies a "hybridization of different feminisms" (Stanford Friedman 2001: 26). Her gendering of Kanackness creates a "nodal point of different cultural backgrounds and geo-political positions" (Gutiérrez Rodríguez 2003: 27).

And it is important not to miss how the dimension of class plays into this. In fact, her intellectual achievements should not be seen as something incidental or extraneous, but as part and parcel of her aesthetics. In her work *Intellectual Migrant Women*, Gutiérrez Rodríguez shows how migration has entailed for intellectual women a process of de-qualification. Manifesting itself as a form of institutionalized ethnicization, declassing translates for intellectual migrant women often into precipitous downward social mobility brought about by means of invalidation of their educational background. "'Being a Turkish woman'," Gutiérrez Rodríguez writes, "denotes not only the construction of a 'different, undeveloped, and unemancipated woman', but it also circumscribes the experiences of declassing in the labor market" (Gutiérrez Rodríguez 1999b: 174). With this in mind, LBR's aesthetically instrumentalized intellectualism—she calls herself "Dr. Bitch Ray"—comments on and subverts these historically manifested practices of declassing. Her emphasis on her academic career thus makes possible her multilayered deconstruction of the image of 'Turkish' woman in Germany. This means, her portrayal of an intellectual Kanackin merges discursively disparate images and thereby puts stress on the gendering and classing of ethno-cultural boundaries. As she says, education is a "weapon" for migrant and working class women: "the only chance of rescue" (Lady Bitch Ray, 2008).

In fact, LBR's image of an intellectual Kanackin avoids typecasting ethnic ascriptions as well as assimilationist connotations—"I'm neither German, nor Turkish" (Lady Bitch Ray 2009). This disassociation from binary positioning is reminiscent of a statement by the 90s rap group Agitpop: "we are not Turks, we are not Germans, we are we. And we have to slowly begin to define who we are" (Der Spiegel 1995). In this respect, the label 'kanak' forms a position beyond clear-cut natio-ethno-cultural boundaries. It functions as a conceptual reversal of a term that emerged in Germany's colonial past and curiously re-entered popular discourse in late 1950s as a denigrating label against male guest workers from Turkey in particular (Adelson 2000; Seidel-Arpacı 2003). Kien NgHi Ha defines this process as "self-kanakization" (Selbst-Kanakisierung)—a form of placing oneself within-yet-against the logic of being always-already labeled as a 'kanak'. As a slur, the term has always borne references to a guest worker existence and connotations of hypermasculinity, reducing male migrant workers, particularly those who came from Turkey, to embodiments of mere "labor power" (Toker 1993: 115).[8] Therefore, despite its positive value of reappropriation, as a postmigrantional vernacular, self-kanakization remained a largely male-centric phenomenon. For instance, Feridun Zaimoglu's 1995 book Kanak Sprak, and more contemporary films such as Kurz und Schmerzlos (1998), Kanak Attack (2000) and Knallhart (2006) carried with them, and to a certain extent reinforced, a history of ethnicized and classed hypermasculinization.[9] They display that, "what is at stake" in the process of self-kanakization, is primarily the link between "masculinity and agency" (Yildiz 2012: 184). For this reason, German speaking minority feminists have drawn attention to the absence of the struggle of marginalized female and queer voices in attempts of empowering migrant positionalities (Yildiz 2004; Steyerl 2001; Gutiérrez Rodríguez 2001, Weber 2005).[10]

---

8   For an extensive analysis of this, also see: Minnaard 2008: 143–178.
9   For an extensive analysis of these movies and their use of the term kanak see: Stehle 2012: 66–126.
10 In an epigraph to an interview with Susan, 29, interpreter of German and English, Zaimoglu reflects on this critique by stating, "[s]he reached me

Recognizing the shortcomings of his Kanak Sprak's gender politics, Feridun Zaimoglu compiled a collection of interviews with women of Turkish cultural background, entitled Koppstoff. In contrast to Kanak Sprak, Koppstoff aimed to document the use of kanak identities from female perspectives "to deconstruct gendered expectations of the victimized female Other" (Stehle 2012: 48). Zaimoglu emphasized this by feminizing the term 'kanak'—as Koppstoff's subtitle reads: Kanaka Sprak. The term 'kanaka', however, failed to take hold in feminist activist, academic, and popular discourse and, strangely enough, the feminizing "a" at the end of the term has been erased for the most recent edition of the book.[11] It took ten years after the publication of Koppstoff, until the release of Ozgur Yildirim's 2008 film Chiko (in which LBR plays the strong, self-assertive prostitute Meryem, who is both sexually and otherwise in charge in her relationship with the male main character), before the image of the kanaka made it into wider pop culture.

By referring to herself as 'Kanackin', LBR feminizes the process of self-kanakization. She does, however, not just rehearse Zaimoglu's label kanaka. In fact, the change of the suffix—from the Spanish -a to the German -in—is by no means coincidental, as it signals participation in a specific Western German feminist history, drawing on a "long struggle" to "achieve visibility for women through feminizing language" (Ferree 2012: 166). And she expands this linguistic intervention with her use of queer-sensitive underscores. In Bitchism, for instance, she frequently refers to a community of "Kanack_innen"

---

over the publication house. She accused me of glorifying typical Turkish machismo and of ignoring the struggle of Turkish-German women in my book *Kanak Sprak*. I suggested interviewing her for a protocol for the Kanaka book" (Zaimoglu [1998] 2011: 146).

11 While the subtitle for the first edition of *Koppstoff* in 1998 reads *Kanaka Sprak vom Rande der Gesellschaft*, the subtitle for the 2011 edition reads *Kanak Sprak: Vom Rande der Gesellschaft*.

(Bitchsm 2012: 345).[12] In this respect, linguistically and performatively, she actualizes what Antke Engel describes as a "queer-feminist and kanakisch attack on the nation" (Engel 1999).

It is in this queer-feminist sense in which she uses the term "Bitchismo," a feminist variant of 'machismo' (LBR 2012b: 435).[13] Evoking strategies explored by Chicana-feminists, LBR's Bitchismo is not only a critique towards gendered colonialist cultural differences. She uses the colonialist idiom that establishes the other culture as 'oppressive' and 'patriarchal'. Therefore, Bitchismo does not necessarily reject all defining characteristics of machismo—aggressiveness, assertiveness, persistence—but it re-uses and feminizes these characteristics in order to develop an embodiment a decolonial feminist empowerment.

---

12 In Germany's feminist intervention, this underscore, unlike other forms of linguistic gender inclusion, not on the condition of two sexes. Rather, sex is thought and visualized as a continuum between male and female, creating a seemingly infinite number of genders (cf. Herrmann 2005).

13 In their book *La Chicana*, Alfredo Mirandé and Evangelina Enriquez describe redefinitions of machismo as forms of political resistance against stereotyping ethnicization (Mirandé/Enriquez 1981: 242). Accordingly, it is "the physical and spiritual conquest" by white Anglo colonizers that "gave rise to the cult of machismo" (ibid: 241). As a result of humiliating and patronizing treatment towards Mexicans, machismo emerged as "a futile attempt to proves one's masculinity" (ibid).

Image 6: LBR as quasi-shemale

Resource: www.ladybitchray.com

Re-located in postmigration and postcolonial ghettoscapes, Bitchismo indicates more than just "a mimetic adaptation to manhood" (Lady Bitch Ray 2012b: 435). Her image of an independent, quick-witted, swaggering persona is inspired by US Black feminist rappers, most notably, Lil' Kim, who not only rid the word 'bitch' of its negative connotations, but redefined its meaning as "positive in the extreme" (Thomas 2009: 51). In Lil Kim's bitch-persona,

> "[t]he tables of domination are turned, overturned or subverted, as she turns phrase after phrase to overthrow the established order of sex, gender and sexuality with a militant resolve. This is her eternal preoccupation in Hip-Hop, this tricksterism. The work of sexual poetic justice is her raison d'être, obviously and all times, her reason-for-being in rhyme." (ibid: 42)

Adopting Lil Kim's sexual poetic of justice, LBR's embodiment of the Kanackin galvanizes a form of transnational empathy.

By casting the Kanackin as a ghetto bitch, she endows Neuer Feminismus with a pronounced "translocal power," establishing an affective bond: a "political idea of kinship that is all the more valuable for its distance" and not originating from "either shared blood or shared land" but from shared experiences (Gilroy 2010: 92). The gathering topos for this affective bond is the ghetto which enables power from below, constructed as a 'not-yet-gentrified', 'not-yet-commodified' space of supposedly authentic cultural production. As a travelling, shifting concept, the ghetto "conjures images from the past: Jewish ghettos, genocide, and Nazi racism" (Stehle 2012: 12). Bearing a history of racialized segregation, in the US, the term ghetto has been used primarily for Black and Puerto Rican districts and their narrative markers: crime, prostitution, poverty, unemployment. In this revised meaning (and being stripped of its Nazi past), the term returned to Germany, now applied to postmigration neighborhoods.[14] In the late 1970s and early 80s, the 'ghetto' underwent further revaluation, becoming associated with a rhetoric of self-empowerment and gritty, street-style coolness.

It is this empowering coolness that forms the affective bond performed by the ghetto bitch, who stands for female voices that rise up despite social segregation, financial hardship, sexist treatments, and violence within and against the community. Or, as LBR puts it, the bitch stands up against the "doppelten Schwanzstrukturen" (twofold dick-structures) (Lady Bitch Ray 2012b: 345). The Hip-Hop feminist bitch generates its own form of 'authentic' cultural production vis-à-vis the male-centric, misogynist rap scene.[15]

Yet, LBR's linking of female Kanackness with the term 'bitch' does not just refer to Black and Hip-Hop feminist street vernacular, but forms a larger transnational empathy: it sheds light on a shared

---

14 A 1973 article with the title "Die Türken kommen: Rette sich wer kann," (The Turks are coming: Save yourself if you can) published in *Der Spiegel*, reveals this shift in rhetoric. It describes Turkish neighborhoods as "ghettos" that alarmingly portend the "downfall of the cities, increased criminality, and social misery like that found in Harlem" (Göktürk et al. 2007: 110).

15 The term Hip-Hop feminism was coined by Joan Morgan. Referring to prominent black feminist MCs, she describes Hip-Hop feminism as "the magical intersection where contrary voices meet—the juncture where 'truth' is no longer black and white but subtle, intriguing shades of gray" (Morgan 1999: 62).

history of ethno-sexualized denigration. In other words, overturning the meaning of 'the bitch' and 'kanakifying' it represents also a locationally specific rhetorical retribution. This is because, in a specific period of German colonialism, around the turn of the twentieth century, being a female 'kanak' was linked to unrestrained, raw sexuality. As many reports and travelogues from German East African colonial projects illustrate, Black women, who were also referred to as 'kanak women' (Kanakenfrau), were denigrated as 'whores' (Huren) (Oguntoye and Ayim 1986: 37). During the Nazi regime this discourse was expanded, stigmatizing "mothers of Afro-Germans, Sinti-Germans, or half-Jewish children," who were "excluded from the cult of [German] motherhood" (ibid: 56).

Moreover, the rhetorical retribution LBR performs by calling herself a 'bitch' gains a particular bend with her self-ethnicization. Marking herself as 'orospu' (Turkish for bitch), she transgresses ethnicized symbolic boundaries of normative constructions of 'Turkish womanhood'.[16] This can be seen as an attempt to forestall and resist forms of gendered denigration and stigmatization. In fact, the force of resistance comes with her insistence, that is, her repetition of the term bitch/orospu/hure. Integrating 'bitch' in her artistic pseudonym, she literalizes the power of self-appellation, as, by speaking about her, one virtually cannot escape but has to utter the abject term. Moreover, the glaring display of words like 'bitch' and 'Votze' (a stylized version of Fotze, which means cunt in German) printed, stitched, and iron-patched on her clothing, and their prominence in her lyrics and her writing constructs an aesthetic of an absurd, almost compulsive, repetition. She creates

---

16 Analyzing one of her Turkish-German participants' statements on the process of ethnicized stigmatization, Gutiérrez Rodríguez notes how "the insult bitch" operates as a discourse that regulates the "dominant gender relations" tied to models of "'national authenticity'" (Gutiérrez Rodríguez 1999b: 188).

"[...] scene of agency from ambivalence, a set of effects that exceed the animating intentions of the call. To take up the name that one is called is no simple submission to prior authority, for the name is already unmoored from prior context, and entered into the labor of self-definition. The word that wounds becomes an instrument of resistance in the redeployment that destroys the prior territory of its operation. Such a redeployment means speaking words without prior authorization and putting into risk the security of linguistic life, the sense of one's place in language, that one's words do as one says. That risk, however, has already arrived with injurious language as it calls into question the linguistic survival of the one addressed. Insurrectionary speech becomes the necessary response to injurious language, a risk taken in response to being put at risk, a repetition in language that forces change." (Butler 1997: 163)

TRANSLINGUALIZATIONS

In fact, LBR's insurrectional speech is based on the already existing ambivalence of the word 'oruspu'. In *Bitchsm*, she recounts anecdotes from her childhood about women living in her childhood neighborhood, who affectionately called each other 'orospu.' She remembers, for instance, how a friend of her mother's used the word as an ironic appellation: "Ne yapiyorsun, kiz Oruspi" (how are you doing, bitch) (Lady Bitch Ray 2012b: 438). Her mother, too, often used the word, albeit in a slightly different context, when she was angry with her children. It is this transgressively ironic, de-tabooing application of the word that constitutes "the bedrock of Bitchsm," as LBR explains (ibid: 438). Her Bitchsm thus excavates alternative meanings of feminist linguistic re-negotiations. That is to say, her sexually explicit language as insurrectional speech emerges with an "affective reworking" of linguistic memory (Yildiz 2012: 147). This evokes a passage in Turkish-German writer Sevgi Özdamar's novel *Life is a Caravanserai* in which the protagonist's mother praises her daughter's wittiness by calling her "a mouth whore, someone who whores with her tongue" (Özdamar 2000, 87). And the narrator perceives this as a compliment: "OROSPU," she exclaims, "I liked the word orospu" (ibid: 87). Similarly stressing her mother's role in the construction of a re-coded feminist idiom, LBR defines her Neuer Feminismus in terms of what Özdamar calls Mutterzunge (1990).[17] In her search for a new feminist discourse, LBR reworks her mother's tongue, which is not necessarily her mother tongue. Her Mutterzunge operates as a citational intervention that translingualizes the 'German' feminist lexicon.[18]

It is necessary to open larger brackets here and revisit the discussion on the mother-daughter dynamics touched upon earlier in this chapter. The important point to note is that the mother-daughter dynamics at play in Özdamar's and LBR's modes of articulation differ from Ute Gehard's formulation. In contrast to the depiction of an in-

---

17 The term Mutterzunge literally translates the Turkish word 'anadil' (mother tongue) into German. In fact, the equivalent of the word 'mother tongue' in German is Muttersprache. In her use of Mutterzunge instead of the word Muttersprache, Özdamar engages in a word play. According to Yildiz, "'mother tongue' is highly ideological, charged, and misleading term" since "it constitutes a condensed narrative about origin and identity" (2012, 12). Özdamar's term Mutterzunge, however, describes a defamiliarizing linguistic constellation that frees one from a monolithic form of belonging. It defamiliarizes by merging and confusing two languages (ibid, 143-168).

18 Here the term 'translingualization' indicates "the process by which new words, meanings, discourses, and modes of representation arise, circulate, and acquire legitimacy within" one language "due to, or in spite of, its contact/collosion with" another (Lui 1995: 26). The translingual is "the very site [...] where the irreducible differences between" these two languages are "fought out," and where "authorities" are "invoked and challenged, ambiguities dissolved or created" (ibid: 26). In this sense, rather than being a mere language crossing, it indicates a rhetorical, discursive and historical intervention into monolingual politics of representation.

escapable, quasi-oedipal logic built into feminism's history, which, as I argue, risks silencing and ignoring migrant and diaspora feminisms, the generational links drawn by Özdamar and LBR offer pathways to decolonize feminist language in Germany. They represent strategic links that point to gaps in the feminist archive.[19] In these links, the established relation between mother and daughter brings to light otherwise submerged and unacknowledged subjectivities through a feminization of (post)migration memory in Germany. These motherdaughter dynamics should therefore be seen as a methodological path for the narration of experiences that have historically been occluded. That is, it gives voice to those who, "through racialization [...] are constructed by the official discourse as 'objects', but not 'agents' of knowledge" (Gutiérrez Rodríguez 2010b: 56).

This is what LBR alludes to when she says that "Kanack women" are seen "as not emancipated" and "needy" (Lady Bitch Ray 2012b: 351). Mocking the view of, in her words, "Nichtkanacken," she goes on: "we German women will show you [how emancipation works], since we've been emancipated long ago" (ibid: 351). With this, she recalls the critique voiced by migrant and minority queer feminists in the early 1990s. Facing the fact that their struggle against racism, homophobia, and class-related inequalities remained largely absent in German feminist agendas, these migrant and minority queer feminists became increasingly active to push the feminist paradigm beyond gender as its sole determinant. The tenor of their critique concerned the prejudice against feminists of different social and cultural backgrounds, who, despite their claims to cultural agency, were trapped in an image of backwardness and thus treated as objects of feminist missionary projects. "Acting like social workers," many German feminists disregarded other claims to feminist agency, picturing non-German women as "backward, isolated and needy" (Ferree 2012:

---

19 Another perfect visual example for this is Seyhan Derin's 1996 film I am my Mother's Daughter, which cinematically works through the filmmaker's mother's memory, unearthing lost experiences of migration.

100–101). As Natasha Apostolidou writes: "[t]he German women in social work have to think about how they can get away from just helping, advising, showing. They have to figure out what kind of power foreign women have, so that they can solidarize with them" (1980: 146). In fact, this confusion and misinterpretation, in rhetoric and practice, began when "the distinction between feminist projects and social work blurred" around 1975-1985 in West Germany (Ferree 2012: 108).

In her article, "Turkish Women, West German Feminists," Rita Chin explores exactly this rhetorical shift and its role in practices of otherization. Drawing on an extensive compilation of work published by West German feminist scholars and activists, Chin demonstrates how these academic works participate in silencing voices of migrant women (Chin 2010). From the perspective of those feminists, the patriarchal structure of migrant, particularly Turkish, women tended to represent "a hindrance to integration" due to supposedly oppressive cultural codes such as "honor" and familial "responsibilities" (White 1997: 758). [20] An example for this view can be found in the introduction that German feminist Susanne von Paczensky wrote for the anthology Frauen aus Anatolia (1978):

"Turkish women now live in our cities as inassimilable, strange bodies. It is no wonder that they provoke prejudice.[...] They walk humbly two steps behind their husbands, and even relinquish the particular domain of women— shopping for food and clothes—to their husbands or children. They contradict every imaginable image of woman: they do not do justice to the traditional role of an efficient mother, who self-confidently manages the household,

---

20 This goal, according to White, 'integration' was represented as achievable by "extracting Turkish women from family expectations and obligations" (White 1997: 758). White underlines the fact that this "German hope" of women emancipation was primarily "reflected in social work literature" (ibid: 759).

much less do they meet emancipated demands in their own ways of life" (cited in Chin 2010: 566).

These 'strange', 'oppressed' bodies provided an image vis-à-vis which West German feminism could assert its emancipatory power. In Helma Lutz's words, "[e]vidence suggests that the ideas and images of 'our' Western femininity are virtually constituted over the delimitation of the Western woman against the Oriental" (Lutz 1999: 149). The construction of the Western emancipated woman in Germany rests on "the daily reconstruction of oppression and backwardness of Islamic women" (ibid: 149). Drawing on Lutz's account, Sedef Gümen explains that, while the image of the "modern, emancipated Western woman is equally a construction," it was primarily the migrant woman who was subject to scrutiny and empirical and social analyses ([1998] 2007: 157). This approach "mystified and dehistoricized" 'German' womanhood by normativizing it and positioning it as meta-categorical over and against 'non-German' others (Gümen 1996, 80).

While migrant women were perceived as not-yet emancipated Orientals, their daughters have been depicted as being in need of 'protection', even 'rescue' from their 'oppressive' families. As if trapped between two different worlds—between their parents' restrictive traditions and 'modern' German society, they are discursively positioned as if they suffer from a deep 'cultural conflict', as embodiments of the clash of civilizations, so to speak. This portrays them as having to get rid of their familial relations in the attempt to attain proper status of 'Western' womanhood. Their supposed inner cultural conflict therefore signifies an "emancipatory conflict, a conflict between forced adherence to the role of the victim, or the 'liberating' adoption of the aspired role of Western European woman" (Otyakmaz 1999: 80). Embarking on a mission to 'save' young women, "Western feminists not only ignored the resistance strategies formulated by emigrants themselves; they also offered solutions [...] that often cut women off from their families and immediate support networks" (Chin 2010: 569).

While the debate foregrounds their familial structures as the root of the problem, the discriminatory attitudes towards these young women in Germany have largely remained unchallenged. In fact, rather than being a solution, cutting off their relations with their families could in many circumstances lead as well to existence in social isolation. African feminist Ifi Amadiume has pointed out how certain traditions can be protective against the patriarchic, sexually abusive, and gender biased structures of 'modern' society (2003: 91). Similarly Turkish-German feminist Neval Gültekin writes:

"If a foreign woman complains about certain troubles or even repression in the family, the European women in most cases wish that she would make herself independent. This kind of self-sufficiency, however, often means flight from the family, loneliness, and a hopeless situation for foreign women and girls. . . For the majority of woman emigrants, the family plays the biggest role in the foreign society . . . If they disown it, they lose every contact to the community" (cited in Chin 2010: 569).

In other words, the promise of emancipation and liberation put forth by German feminists and social workers does by no means imply "full membership" in German society (White 1997: 760). Furthermore, if there is any conflict these young women encounter, it cannot be reduced to mere cultural incompatibility. As Otyakmaz's study Auf Allen Stühlen (1994). demonstrates, rather than being caught in between, young German-Turkish women fuse and conjoin different cultural positions .What troubles them instead is rather a limited societal understanding of 'belonging' that imposes an either/or paradigm. "Some tend to think," Amadiume remarks, "that the choices for feminist roles without rejection of traditional culture are very limited. This would suggest an assumption that feminism and traditional culture are mutually exclusive" (2003: 102).

PRODUCTIVE PARADOXES

LBR's Neuer Feminismus questions this antithetical relation between feminism and traditional culture. She toys with this tension when she says that she would raise her children in accordance with 'Turkish' norms and values, claiming that she would tell her daughter: "I don't want you to have a boyfriend at 16," because, as she reasons, "happiness is not defined by way of evermore relationships" (Lady Bitch Ray 2006). However contradictory it might seem, especially regarding its rather pronounced gender bias, this statement captures the way she entangles supposedly oppositional discourses. While seemingly embodying Western ideals of emancipation—nudity, sexual explicitness, promiscuity—the vocabulary she draws on connotes a traditionalist view associated with 'Turkish' culture in Germany. Her use of a stereotypically conservative gender bias sensationalizes her rhetoric and creates a confusing image, positioning her in mutually opposed discourses, traditionalist and feminist at the same time.

In this respect, her performance also reveals the paradox inherent in the discourse of modernization, that is, its own normativity and impermeability despite its ideals of tolerance and equal participation. She expresses this by saying, "only modern Turks are accepted [in Germany], but then again, with my moral values, I do not belong to those either" (Lady Bitch Ray 2013). While rejecting the assimilationist spin of the word 'modern', she nevertheless defines the "ideal kanack-bitch" as "a modern, self-determined woman of Turkish origin with rebellious blood in her veins" (Lady Bitch Ray 2012b: 345). How can we read her critical use of 'modern' in one statement and her endorsement of the same concept in the other? Amadiume's deconstruction of the concept once again might be of help here. Whereas in the first statement, LBR equates 'modern' with assimilated and subordinated, in the second, she describes those who are "appropriating and adapting traditional practices to their needs" (Amadiume 2003, 103). This becomes more clear with her description of the "kanack-Bitch-identity" as a composition of "old and new elements"

(Lady Bitch Ray 2012b, 348). To re-cite Anzaldúa's conceptualization of the new mestiza, the 'kanack-bitch' "take[s] inventory [...]. She reinterprets history and, using new symbols, she shapes new myths" (Anzaldúa 1987: 82).

Similar to her treatment of the word 'bitch', she shows a certain unfaithfulness towards the established use of the word 'modern'. Yet again, she does not attempt to radically reverse concepts. Because the words she uses acquire multiple, at times, oppositional, and contradictory meanings, she opens up language in the sense of what Walter Mignolo calls "epistemic disobedience" (2009). According to Mignolo, rather than an outright rejection of Western concepts and knowledges, epistemic disobedience is the effort to recast them, loosen and proliferate their meanings and activate "the repository of concepts, energies and visions that have been reduced to silences or absences" (Mignolo 2007: 485). And one of the most triumphalist concepts tied to the ideal of progress and comfortably seated in the rhetoric of Western modernity is the "rational concept of emancipation" (ibid: 454). In fact, "Westernization" as such, as Nilüfer Göle puts it, "is a condition of women's emancipation," which brings in questions as to what extent feminism is linked to a history of epistemic colonialism (1996: 6).

To untie it, expand its discursive reach, and open it up for feminisms that move beyond Western-oriented language, emancipation has to be confronted with its opposite, that is, with what is constructed as not emancipation. For the restricting dimension of the Western feminist use of emancipation tends to be bound up with the rhetoric of secularism and sexual freedom. Possibilities of intervention and rhetorical proliferation thus involve the question of how feminist emancipation can be embodied differently.

Referring to Turkish-German women, Otyakmaz states, "norms and values of the culture of origin are implicitly or explicitly juxtaposed in opposition to German culture, which supposedly grants more opportunities for emancipation and independence as well as sexual self-determination" (Otyakmaz 1999: 79). Being a feminist thus carries with it specific terms of emancipation. Probing the Western-centric context of feminism in Germany and shedding light on the link between Western feminist rhetoric of emancipation and cultural otherization, German-Turkish feminist Gültekin asks tauntingly, "assimilation to emancipation?" (1986). Gültekin remarks that "the local women only accepted those of us who are 'emancipated', which meant for many of us to first renounce our [cultural] backgrounds" (ibid: 93). According to Gültekin, "amongst the young emigrants who grew up here, self-renunciation has often been (mis)understood as an accomplishment on the way towards emancipation, which nevertheless did not save them from persistent discrimination" (ibid: 93). And the way to emancipation for these women has not just been defined by way of disassociation from non-Western cultural backgrounds but also by way of fulfillment of certain feminist criteria. Moving the issue of sexual freedom to the center of its agenda of emancipation, 'German' feminism has positioned migrant women as being sexually suppressed. For this reason, "feminist movements in other parts of the world and emancipatory strategies of migrant women here are gauged against the Western Women movement and devalued as not sufficiently feminist, or have no visibility at all" (Otyakmaz 1995, 20). Precisely speaking, the problem was therefore not necessarily that other modalities of emancipation went unheeded, but that alternative emancipatory positionalities were cloaked and barred by the monocultural stance of 'German' feminism, which has defined itself over and against the other woman.

LBR hints at this latent ethnicization of gender politics in Germany. Though, at first glance, she might seem to unquestionably affirm and glorify the rhetorical tradition of Western feminism, she also reveals its limitation, that is, its limiting means of emancipation. In her view, the rhetorical constraint that results from binding emancipation to images of unrestricted sexuality has produced an "attitude of superiority of the German woman" (Überlegenheitsattitüde des deutschen Weibs) vis-à-vis the "kanack women" (Kanackenfrauen) (Lady Bitch Ray 2012b: 351). For her, it is "a fallacy" to portray "acted-out sexuality and freedom—like excessive consumption of alcohol or frequent change of sexual partners" as the sole "indicators of emancipation" (ibid: 351). In the same passage, she states that "freedom" does not come with "degenerate sexuality." Her word choice is significant here, as it paradoxically invokes a discourse seen as conservative, backward, and oppressive, and essentializingly associated with Turkish culture. Like Otyakmaz, she reminds us that "not for all women [...] must sexual freedom be the most important goal" (Otyakmaz 1995: 20). Delinking emancipation from sexual freedom, she pushes for a feminist discourse beyond the Western-centric, secular-modernist paradigm. Referring to her doctoral thesis on the semiotics of the headscarf, she points out that being a Muslim woman involves following "certain rules, such as having no pre-martial sex. However, they also expect their potential partners to obey such rules. And that is emancipation!" (Lady Bitch Ray 2014). Rather than an individualist body politics of 'sexual freedom', emancipation is here recast in terms of an equality of requirements.[21] For her, a decolonization of feminist rhetoric in Germany means loosening the signifying ties of emancipation. Her sexual explicitness does therefore not just parody and objectifying male gaze. While drawing on a Western feminist tradition that tackled the fetishization of the female body by using rather than rejecting sexual explicitness, she also reveals the link between Western modernist emancipation and a normative, culturally 'assimilated'/'integrated' mode of feminist embodiment.

That is why her sexual explicitness along with her self-ethnicization exposes cultural boundaris of emancipation. Because it entangles feminist rhetoric in paradoxes of emancipation, her ethnicized sexual explicitness toys with a mode of unveiling that, as an epistemological practice, guides Western (post)modernity. Gaining force with the Enlightenment, the Western project of modernization is marked by a rationalist drive towards visibility and empirical verifia-

---

21 In my group discussions, the participants conceptualized emancipation in a similar manner. See chapter 3.

bility. Everything undisclosed, covered and concealed tends to become suspicious—an urge for transparency that Spivak has called "clarity fetishism" (in Braidotti 2011: 204). LBR's ambiguous resistance against an ethnicizing/exoticizing gaze on other femininities bears similarities to Fanon's description of Algerian women's defiance against the dress codes and regimes of embodiment imposed by the French colonizers. According to Fanon, to mock and mislead their colonial 'emancipators', many Algerian women acted as if they complied with the colonialist project of 'emancipation' and unveiled themselves, only to carry out their resistance more surreptitiously, circumventing the suspicious the gaze of the occupiers (Fanon 1967: 35-67).

Fanon's disentangling of the other's body's status as being veiled found an early articulation in DuBois' The Souls of Black Folk (Du Bois [1903] 2007). As exoticized objects of a colonial gaze, DuBois argues, Blacks are shrouded in a myth of otherness, which is, in his analysis, paradoxically a curse and a blessing—the former because of racial typecasting (and segregation) and the latter because of the ability to ambiguously identify with and transgress racialized symbolic boundaries. For DuBois, racialized subjects "possess [...] agency [...] in taking" the veil "on and off" (Blau/S. Brown 2001: 221).

To stay with DuBoisian terms, LBR's rebelliousness takes shape not just because of sexually explicit imagery and rhetoric, but because she ambiguously positions herself "within and without the veil" (DuBois [1903] 2007: 8). In her merging of the 'traditional' with the 'modern', the meaning of emancipation is decentered. She seems to confound what does and what does not count as emancipation, which also sparks questions as to the history of the embodiment of 'Turkish' womanhood in Germany. Deniz Camlikbeli's remark in 1984 points to ethnicized gendered dress codes: "the Turkish woman is not the prototype of oppression and suffering because she wears a headscarf, and the German woman is not the prototype of self-determination because she walks around topless" (1984:19).[22] One could expand this formulation to a larger discursive entanglement of Turkish womanhood with 'being oppressed'. That is to say, Turkishness (and in fact, cultural otherness and Muslim culture particularly) is always-already positioned within the veil, regardless of whether or not actual markers like the headscarf are present. There is a liability, a certain burden of proof on the side of cultural others. This manifests itself, for instance, in the citizenship test, which assesses applicants in terms of their fitness for Western secular democracy. As Yasemin Yildiz argues, the questions of the citizenship test suggest that the applicants are presumed to be backward, religiously orthodox, and intolerant (Yildiz 2011). Positioned within the veil, cultural others are supposed to demonstrate their 'tolerance'. Westernization therefore requires a certain rhetorical self-unveiling.

LBR's form of unveiling, however, goes far beyond the requirements imposed on culturally 'different' subjects. Tellingly, she was censored, and, in fact, fired, by Radio Bremen and her scholarship at a leftist foundation in Germany was suspended based on her 'offensive' rhetoric and 'inappropriate' appearance on TV shows. In order to have her scholarship resumed, she had to explain the "feminist message" of her performance to a committee (Lady Bitch Ray 2012: 453). As she writes in *Bitchsm*, she was also at risk of being exmatriculated because of numerous complains submitted by journalists and university authorities. The degree of her sexual explicitness therefore points to the moral boundaries of the dominant culture. Because it borders on the 'sittenwidrig' (indecent), her representation

---

22 The original German version reads: "Die Türkische Frau ist nicht der Prototyp der Unterdrückung und des Leidens, weil sie ein Kopftuch trägt, und die deutsche Frau ist nicht der Prototyp der Selbsbestimmmung, weil sie oben ohne geht." Camlikbeli's expression "oben ohne" has a double meaning in this context. On the one hand, one can read it as 'without headscarf', or in the conventional usage of the phrase, meaning 'half-naked'.

reverses the condition of being tested, highlighting dominant cultural censorship. Hers is a strategic unveiling, revealing the dubious divisions based on 'tolerance' pointing to the limits of Western 'emancipation'.

By positioning herself paradoxically with respect to the polarized provinces of emancipation, LBR engages in re-shaping feminist activism in Germany. She recalibrates feminist rhetoric for a postmigration setting, weaving in unacknowledged feminist experiences, shedding light on feminists' (m)other('s) tongue. That is, she translingualizes and complicates popfeminism in Germany. Straddling multiple axes of difference, her Neuer Feminismus merges transnational narratives with situated local histories. As a 'Kanackin', she poses questions as to who is entitled to represent 'emancipation' and probes the feminist activist dilemma of either universalism or particularism, that is, of either global sameness or essentializing difference. In other words, her art suggests that, to be politically effective, feminist activism, in whatever form, does not have to, and perhaps even should not, be in total harmony with an already existing set of vocabulary. It is not about diplomatic settlements of compromises, but rather about an embrace of the sometimes uncomfortable contradictions that do not seem to make sense, unless one slackens and unhinges the frame of one's feminism. Reaching out for a transcultural form of activism, her sexual explicitness tests the limits of the established concept of emancipation, diverting, bending and stretching feminist embodiments in Germany.

Image 6: LBR in 'Fick Workout' costume

Situational Analysis of the Group Discussions
Notes on Methods and Methodologies

In the forgoing part, I engaged in an interpretation of Lady Bitch Ray's performance with respect to gendered ethno-cultural positionalities. This chapter examines the group discussions in which the participants discussed Lady Bitch Ray's music video "Du Bist Krank." The group discussions consist of students at the University of Kassel, whose parents or grandparents migrated from Turkey to Germany. I consider working with these groups as an important aspect of my study, since I see it as creating ways of representation of cultural differences in the realm of higher education where these differences remain largely underrepresented.[1] I employed focus group discussions so as to foreground the dialogical and interactive mode of interpretation (Morgan 1997; Kitzinger/Barbour 1999; Krueger/Casey 2000; Bloor 2001; Liamputtong 2011). As Jenny Kitzinger notes, "[f]ocus groups are discussions organized to explore a specific set of issues

---

1 As Gutierrez Rodriguez maintains, compared to British universities, German universities eschew a comprehensively inclusive recruitment policy, especially when it comes to members of "local minorities" (2010b, 58).

such as people's views and experiences" of "a particular set of questions" (Kitzinger 1994: 103). Contrary to the traditional approach to interviews, focus groups concentrate explicitly on interactive communication between the participants (Krueger 1998; Greenbaum 2000). Interaction, for me, is, however, not limited to verbalized articulation, but includes gestures, postures, and the absence of speech. In this sense, I treated the group discussions as "space[s] for a politics of voice that includes silence as part of the interaction" (Moss 2011: 379).

The inter- and intra-active nature of the focus group discussions provided a setting in which the students discussed their experiences and standpoints regarding socio-cultural positioning in postmigration Germany. I am not only interested in how the participants are positioned within (pre)existing discourses, but also in how they creatively and critically deal with and navigate through these discourses. This also means that these focus groups are by no means to be understood as representative case studies of the so-called third generation of German-Turks. On the contrary, I focus primarily on how the gendered representational topoi of 'Germanness' and 'Turkishness' emerge and materialize in the collective experiences situated in the dynamics of the group discussions. Similarly, the central issue of the focus group discussions is not the question of whether the participants actually reached a conclusive opinion or not, but "how knowledge, ideas, story-telling, self-presentation and linguistic exchanges operate within" the discursive setting of the discussions (Kitzenger 1999: 5).[2]

---

[2] Before entering my actual research field, I have conducted two in-depth interviews with one male and one female student and a small focus group discussion with two female students, in which Lady Bitch Ray's music video "Du Bist Krank" was initially shown. A comparison of these diverging methodologies indicated that the interaction between participants in focus groups is of greater service for the complexity of my research topic. In the interviews I conducted, the interviewees largely concentrated on personal accounts such as individual life experiences and anecdotes.

To explore the group dynamics and the participants' interactive mode of argumentation, rather than focusing on individuals per se, I designed my primary research questions as follows: how do the participants position Lady Bitch Ray and themselves with regard to the gendered national categories in contemporary postmigration Germany? How do the participants draw on, appropriate and/or circumvent existing discourses? How does the interplay between the positions shown point to absences and potential emergences of other discursive repertoires?

SITUATIONAL ANALYSIS—MAPS, GAPS, AND TRAPS

We are "in the seventh moment of qualitative inquiry," according to Yvonne Lincoln and Denzin Norman. This moment signals "a pressing need to look back and see what issues we need to bring forward into the new century, what knots can we firmly secure, which knots should be undone, and where new knots might need to be tied" (Lincoln/Denzin 2003: 3). Patricia Leavy suggests "representing research findings in terms of 'shapes'" because shapes do not only chart "the form of our work," but also present "the way [...] the form shapes the content and how that content is received by audiences" (Leavy 2014:

> Relatively little attention was paid to Lady Bitch Ray's performance. Upon clear-cut statements concerning what is 'right' and what is 'wrong' in LBR's performance, the topics quickly shifted to biographical accounts of the participants. In contrast, in the pretest focus group the participants were jointly trying to give meaning to Lady Bitch Ray's performance and recurrently questioned, challenged, and affected each other's arguments. That being the case, it became evident that focus group discussions are the most expedient data gathering method for the subject matter of my research.

725, emphasis in original). Therefore, a focus the knots of gathered data means a "return to the potential shift from 'knowing' to 'relating to' to develop the understanding of the multiplicity of the world/worlds, and the questions raised for the role of methods in not only 'catching' these multiple realities, but making them" (Coleman/Ringrose 2013: 6, emphasis in original). In other words, knots offer "mov[ing] away from seeing individuals as clearly bounded subjects [...] towards a mapping of the relations in which researchers are always involved" (ibid: 6).

In my analysis of the participants' responses to the music video, I used Grounded Theory, and more specifically, Situational Analysis, a variant of Grounded Theory developed by Adele E. Clarke (2005). Clarke's method complicates the process of data analysis by highlighting the multivalencies and incongruities of the research setting. This means, Situated Analysis undermines the presumed autotelic nature of empirical data. Unlike traditional Grounded Theory, Situational Analysis includes discursive and material dynamics in its analytic process as a methodologically integral part, rather than treating them merely as an analytic result. Particular attention is therefore paid to discursive shifts and gaps, which are visualized as part of the empirical dynamics in three types of maps: positional maps, social arenas maps and situational maps.

In line with my research questions, the goal of Situational Analysis concerns "elucidating differences, making silences speak, and revealing contradictions within positions and within groups" (Clarke 2011: 361). Moreover, Situational Analysis becomes helpful "where the desire is to grasp both the specifics of the local situations and the perspectives of local people on their own needs—remembering that these may be multivocal, gendered, and contradictory" (ibid: 361, emphasis in original). Similar to classical Grounded Theory, Clarke's method uses coding as its major analytic tool. The codes and categories collected in the empirical setting, however, are not just seen as indicators of already existing discourses, but also taken as indicators of what is not (yet) codable. To be aware of these moments of uncodability, the researcher has to remain skeptical towards the immediate availability of certain codes and categories. With this methodological self-reflexivity, the researcher focuses not only on what sort of codes are grounded in the empirical setting, but also pays attention to "[w]hat sort of coding has produced the [empirical] subject" (Spivak 1993: 19; my emphasis).

Shaping Discourses, Knitting the *Not Yet*

In her book Situational Analysis: Grounded Theory of the Postmodern Turn (2005), Clarke seeks to disconnect "Grounded Theory from its positivist roots" and adapt it to postmodern understandings of the subject as enacted through "situatedness, variations, differences of all kinds, and positionality/relationality" (Clarke 2005: xxviii). Instead of tidily arranging the collected data, Situational Analysis thoroughly embraces the "messiness and denseness" of empirical results (ibid: xxvii). Whereas classical Grounded Theory is undergirded by a positivist urge to universalize empirical results, Situational Analysis is attentive to the fragmentary, provisional and incomplete dimension of research findings. In Situational Analysis, therefore, "[t]he situation per se becomes the ultimate unit of analysis, and understanding its elements and their relations is the primary goal" (ibid: xxii, emphasis in original). Situational Analysis offers methodologies to create situated theories rather than assuming that 'the truth' is grounded in the data and should be discovered and brought to light by the researcher. In other words, it takes the entire premise of Grounded Theory, that is, the grounding of the data, as an ongoing, research-setting-dependent process.

Clarke draws on Kathy Charmaz's influential Constructing Grounded Theory (2000), which already put Grounded Theory's positivist roots under question by emphasizing empirical study as a process of meaning-making. Charmaz's approach underlines the importance of reevaluating Grounded Theory by "stress[ing] its emergent, constructivist elements" (Charmaz 2000: 510). However, by introducing Situational Analysis, Clarke attempts to move beyond the action-centered vision of empirical research, which still remains determinant in Charmaz's approach. Whereas action-centered Grounded Theory seeks answers to questions as to what is going on, situated analysis aims at making visible the conditions that bring that what is going on into being. According to Clarke, "studying action is not enough" (Clarke 2007: 432). As she suggests, a similar attention should be paid to actors, their discursive positions and the relations between these positions, that is what Clarke calls to the "situational matrix" (idib: 432). The central focus of Situational Analysis is therefore not on "how contextual elements condition [...] action" but how conditions are enacted, that is, how they are actualized in a particular empirical situation (Clarke 2005: xxxv).

Aiming to unground Grounded Theory by moving beyond action, Situational Analysis nevertheless keeps intact Grounded Theory's basic elements such as theoretical sampling, sensitizing concepts, memo writing, open-coding. In fact, particularly open-coding remains crucial because it accommodates multiplicity and fluctuation. It reflects how sets of data are pliable and erratic. For the coding process does not merely order and label the individual's words, but seeks to trace systematically individual and collective articulations of social phenomena. Through segmentation, open-coding first divides the total frame of data into various fragments, and then reassembles these fragments into clusters of meanings and references. It enables the formation of different perspectives onto that what is said by the participants, because it highlights various interconnections and cross-references between the fragments of the collected data. By undoing and differently rearranging the order of the empirical data, it transforms the frame the research conducted into a fragmented whole.

In addition to these basic elements of Grounded Theory, Clarke proposes three main cartographic approaches through which the complexity and entangeldness of the research situation can be visualized. These maps—called social worlds/arenas maps, positional maps and situational (project) maps—are created through analysis of discourses and analysis of positioning. The social worlds/arenas map illustrates narrative clusters become salient in the research setting. "[T]he major task" of the social arenas map is to specify "the key social worlds" that were particularly prominent in the empirical work (Clarke 2005: 112). It demonstrates the "universe of discourses" (ibid: 46). In other words, it gathers the elements of discourses in a broad image by asking "how did the various worlds see and constellate one another" or "what is happening between particular worlds" (ibid: 113; 195). Drawing primarily on Foucault, Clarke states that her use of the concept of discourse is "writ large": it "includes word choice, arguments, warrants, claims, motives and other purposeful, persuasive features of language" (ibid: 148). She also underscores that discourse has other complex and multifaceted dimensions, which means that it cannot be "limited to language" (ibid: 148).[3] As Adam Jaworski and Nikolas Coupland assert "it is language reflecting social order but also language shaping social order, and shaping individuals' interaction with society" (Jaworski/Coupland 1999: 3). Therefore, through the lens of Situational Analysis, the analysis of discourses and positions requires a fine listening and an intertextual interpretation that focuses on verbal as well as non-verbal articulation.

As my study shows, individuals and group members can remain critical and cautious towards the immediately available rhetorical repertoire. It was necessary for me in my study to not only take into account what was directly stated but also the participants' rejection to associate certain meanings with particular concepts (disarticulation), their ironic and repetitive use of particular words (over-articulation), their avoidance of certain terms, and their silences (under-articulation). This approach enabled me to be attentive not only to the discursive limits—'what can and should be said'—but also how these constraints are used productively, that is to say, how the participants

---

3 For the historical and disciplinary view on the concept 'discourse' in both Anglo and German contexts, see: Reiner Keller, *Doing Discourse Research: An Introduction for Social Science*, (2013).

critically and creatively used these discursive boundaries and blind spots (Pecheux 1986: 112). Being alert to how boundaries are traversed and/or circumvented also means being perceptive to emergence, or, to what cannot yet be put in other words. This is why, according to Norman Fairclough, this kind of analysis "can provide particularly good indicators of social change" (Fairclough 1995: 209). Similarly, Clarke underlines that "careful attention to the historical timing of the emergence of new discursive elements and changes in old ones can reveal" potentials "for new ways to construct reality" (Clarke 2005: 151).

In this sense, Clarke's perspective can be compared to what sociologist Boaventura Sousa de Santos calls the "sociology of emergences" (2004). A sociology of emergences aims at a recognition of the gaps created through the process of exclusion and marginalization, that is, how certain knowledges are in fact "disqualified and rendered invisible, unintelligible" (de Sousa Santos 2004: 14).[4] Key to this is the concept of the Not Yet, which, as Santos writes, is "the way in which the future is inscribed in the present. It is not an indeterminate or infinitive future, rather a concrete possibility and a capacity that neither exist in a vacuum nor is completely predetermined" (ibid: 25). Therefore, what is needed for grounding the 'Not Yet' is attention to what remains silent. Hence, Santos proposes what he calls the "sociology of absences," which aims at illuminating "the realities rendered absent by silence, suppression, and marginalization" (de Sousa Santos 2004: 23). In a similar vein, Clarke underlines the importance of charting "what is not there" which, for her, is a way "to explore the silences" (Clarke 2005: 127; 136). Exploring and coding the Not Yet means thus looking beyond that what is immediately accessible and directly encoded, and being sensitive to what is embryonic, latent, submerged or rendered minor.

---

4   Santos borrows the Not Yet from German philosopher Ernst Bloch's concept Noch Nicht (Santos 2004: 25–28).

A primary tool for this is the positional map, which lays out the "positions articulated and not articulated in discourses" (ibid: 86). Since Clarke does not elucidate the dynamics of positionality, a complementary approach can thus be seen in "positioning analysis" which Michael Bamberg defines as an "empirically grounded analysis of how subjects construct themselves by analyzing the positions that are actively and agentively taken in their narratives vis-à-vis normative discourses" (Bamberg 2003: 10). It focuses on how the participants position themselves in relation to their co-participants and the topic at hand by means of "turn taking, topical shifts, contrasts, repairs, lexical and pronoun choice, formulaic expressions, language varieties" (Korobov 2001: para. 26). What is important to emphasize, however, is that the positions illustrated in a map are far from being stable, coherent and independent. Rather they are to be understood as precarious, contradictory and relational. Because they are in movement, they are always problematic. Therefore, it is not that a position as such serves as the primary unit of analysis but positioning, the movement of how positions come into being. It is thus not a question of occupation or even arrival, but rather one of departure and direction: where from and where to. If positioning marks the very movement of discourse, it is equally important to consider the intervals between positions. In this light, empirical focus is not only on the positions that are taken but also on those that are missed, left out, avoided, not recognized, and not acknowledged. As Brian Massumi suggests, rather than creating a clearly defined "grid," positioning should be seen in terms of the passageways through which it moves, or, as he puts it, in terms of "the space of crossing, the gaps between positions on the grid" (Massumi 2002: 4). Positional maps aim to make such passageways visible.

Clarke's third and final map is the situational (project) map. For this map, the researcher creates an abstract image by amalgamating through interpretation social arenas and positional maps. While the social arenas and positional maps help to the researcher to "determine which stories to tell" the situational (project) map "frames th[ese] stor[ies] through mapping the broader situation as a whole and all the elements in it at a more general and abstract level" (Clarke 2005: 111; 137). That is to say, a situational (project) map visualizes the relation between the discourses and the prominent forms of (non)positioning. Since "project maps are project-specific," there is no particular way to tell what counts as a project map or how to create one. However, Clarke emphasizes that "a good picture or a diagram" that captures the sense and the spirit of an empirical work can make the entire project "visually more accessible" (ibid: 288).[5]

Besides expanding traditional Grounded Theory into a more complex analytic frame, Situational Analysis takes into account the fundamental contingency of the research outcomes. Through coding of articulations and categorization of segments with tentative interpretations, it aims at providing provisional narratives rather than offering an overarching interpretive key. And important is not only to create narratives from the empirical data but also to explore the interrelationality and intra-activity of these narratives. By focusing on the dynamics between voice and silence, between the said and the unsaid, presence and absence, Situational Analysis thus offers a deconstructionist Grounded Theory. And in probing these ambiguities, it lends itself to a decolonizing approach to qualitative research. For it encourages the researcher to forgo reduction and simplification and instead embrace the messiness that occurs when certain things cannot be explained through pre-existing, hegemonically imposed models of interpretation. In my project, using Clarke's mapping processes was helpful not to reduce the complexity of my data to a monolithic whole, but instead heed the multiplicity of interpretations produced through a variety of convergences and intersections of discourses.

---

5   I present my analytic maps at the end of this chapter.

Linking Theoretical Sensitivity with Self-Reflexivity

Theoretical sensitivity has always been a defining feature of Grounded Theory. Yet, its meaning underwent various modifications and remains contested. As Barney Glaser and Anselm Strauss's pivotal contribution, theoretical sensitivity set Grounded Theory apart from purely scientific positivism, taking into account the researcher's subjective presence. In their Discovery of Grounded Theory, Glaser and Strauss state that theoretical sensitivity "involves the sociologist's ability to have theoretical insight into his [sic] area of research combined with an ability to make something of his [sic] insights" (Glaser/Strauss 1967: 46). This, however, also indicates the remaining vagueness of their concept, since it describes the notion of theoretical sensitivity as an individual skill of the researcher. In fact, they reduce theoretical sensitivity to a certain knowledge pool that might be tapped during research in order to glean the relevant aspects from the collected data. Moving towards a more constructivist approach, Strauss and Corbin redefined theoretical sensitivity by accepting that both the production of data as well as the generated theories are "interpretations made from given perspectives as adopted or researched by researchers" (Strauss/Corbin 1994: 279). "Sensitivity," Corbin and Strauss maintain in a later work, "is the fascinating interplay of researcher and data in which understanding of what is being described in the data slowly evolves until finally the researcher can say 'Aha, that is what they are telling me'" (Corbin/Strauss 2008: 33). This understanding is nevertheless problematic as it risks mythifying a sudden revelation occurring in the course of analyzing one's data. In my own research, for instance, this defining epiphany never occurred. The expectation of an automatic materialization of the Aha moment might even be counterproductive, since it pushes (especially novice) researchers into overestimations of the aim and capacity of methodology. The view of having an ultimate goal in finding a singular, overarching theory emerging out of the collected data is highly idealistic. In their commentary on Clarke's article, Corbin and Strauss note that Clarke's understanding of theoretical sensitivity posits that "theory does not just 'emerge' from the data; rather, data itself is constructed from many events observed or read about or heard about" (Strauss/Corbin 1997: 64). It is important to bear in mind that, in Situational Analysis, the "actors' own words and interpretations are necessary, respected but recast in new and analytic terms" (ibid: 64). Working with Clarke's expanded understanding of theoretical sensitivity, I believe that tantamount to the 'validity' and 'relevance' of the outcomes is the researcher's reflection on her own positions and perspectives.

During my field research, I sensed my own position as remaining ambiguous, particularly in relation to the research participants. The fact that I was neither born nor raised in Germany in some situations signified cultural difference, especially when it came to topics regarding which the participants' stressed their sense of 'non-belonging' to Turkey.[6] On the other hand, however, my cultural background also highlighted similarities in terms of understanding of certain cultural codes.[7] At times, I was positioned as a researcher from Turkey who came to Germany for educational purposes.[8] I sensed their eagerness to support me to realize my project. Moreover, as they themselves

---

6 In fact, as I show in the next chapter, in my group discussions, 'being born and raised' in Germany bore particularly strong signification of one's belonging.

7 This was most explicitly articulated by the participants' frequent use of the phrase "as you know." Similarly, in her article "Tell me who you are," Dudu Jankie writes how her participants' were positioning her both as an insider and as an outsider during her research project, whereby she reads her participants' expression of "you know" as positioning her as an insider (Jankie 2004: 87–105).

8 This was particularly apparent when the participants used phrases in German. Unprompted, they translated or elaborated on the meaning of their expressions. A couple of times, they translated my expressions to one another.

stressed during the group discussions, my research topic triggered their interest, since it deals with topics they could directly relate to. However, from my own perspective, my position is by no means fixed merely to Turkishness. Living in an Anglo-German-Turkish environment, I myself experience a highly shifting context of cultural references. This experience played a significant role for my way of approaching the collected data, which displayed shifts between languages and various social and political discourses.

GROUNDED THEORY IN MULTILINGUAL RESEARCH—IN-VIVO CODING AND TRANSCULTURAL TRANSLATION

From the early stages of this study, language has been a major challenge and a crucial factor that shaped not only the production of data but also how I approached the data at the interpretive level. During my stay in Nordstadt, a neighborhood in Kassel with a high percentage of people with migration background, I realized that to it was necessary for me to improve my German in order to better communicate with the German-Turkish youth (since they were using a linguistic composite of both German and Turkish). Thus, in order to ease my entry into my field research, I attended a German language course. Being able to speak German, I started to search participants for my research project. Using social media platforms such as StudiVZ and Facebook, I managed to gather my group discussion members within six weeks and the first discussion took place in November 2010 and the last one took place in December 2010. After conducting the last session, I began transcribing the data. A colleague of mine who is a native speaker of both Turkish and German translated the first discussion to German.[9] Since especially the first group discussion showed a bilingual atmosphere, translating the Turkish part of the transcript to German minimized the possibility of losing meaning in the process of translation.[10] In order to keep the bilingual aspect of the data visible, I italicized the German expressions in the excerpts to leave for the reader visual traces of the bilingual spirit of the discussions.

I kept the other two group discussions' transcripts in the original (Turkish-German), and translated to English only the excerpts I selected to present in the dissertation. After the transcription and translation process, involving English during the interpretation and writing stage further emphasized the role of language and, in fact, produced a trilingual framework for this study. Since I used the German version of the first group discussion's transcription in the interpretation groups I joined, I also used the same version for the process of open coding.[11] Yet, while coding, I repeatedly returned to the original audiotape in order to 'fill in' the gaps produced by the translation and/or the transcription.

---

9   At that point, a German translation became necessary in order to make the text available for non-Turkish speaking colleagues with whom I built interpretation groups.
10 In fact, a translation to English would have presented an unnecessary additional 'filtering' of the data.
11 The first group discussion transcript underwent twice a line-by-line opencoding process: first an initial coding, which aims at "remain[ing] open to all possible theoretical direction indicated" by the data, and then an evaluation coding, which aims at grounding the participants' judgmental verbal and non-verbal expressions (Saldaña 2009: 81; 97). After that, all three transcripts underwent three different focus coding processes, which enabled an assessment of the "comparability and transferability" of the data (ibid: 155). Focus coding helped to develop theoretical frameworks by comparing and contrasting the major themes occurring in the three group discussions.

Translanguaging the Coding Process

Rather than adopting a widely used linguistic notion of code-switching, I use Li Wei's concept translanguaging to describe the approach I followed while coding and categorizing my bilingual data (2011). According to Ofelia Garcia and Li Wei, "translaguaging differs from the notion of code-switching" (Garcia/Wei 2014: 22). Wei describes code-switching as occurring "when a bilingual talks to another bilingual with the same linguistic background and changes from one language to another in the course of conversation" (Wei 2013: 33). In contrast to code-switching, translanguaging "considers the language practices of bilinguals not as two autonomous language systems" but rather "as one linguistic repertoire with features that have been societally constructed as belonging to two separate languages" (Garcia/Wei 2014: 2). What makes translanguaging particularly useful for the coding process of my bilingual data is the fact that it does not focus on the speakers' use of grammar but on "the speakers' construction and use of original and complex interrelated discursive practices" that is metaralized with/through the particular linguistic repertoire (ibid: 22).

Critiquing the attempt to generate a common rule or code-switching as a language practice, Benjamin Bailey underlines the fact that "it is not always possible to ascribe any function to a particular switch" (Bailey 2007: 265). Similarly, in his introduction to Code-Switching in Conversation: Language, Interaction and Identity, Peter Auer points to the risk of ascribing an overarching logic to these kinds of language switches, since "what linguists tend to take for granted as 'codes' [...] may not be looked upon as codes by participants" (Auer 2002a: 2). Elsewhere, Auer draws attention to the fact that "[b]ilingual talk cannot be analyzed as a mixture of two monolingual codes" (Auer 2007: 334). This means, "the starting point of bilingual analyses can no longer be two languages, but rather a collection of discursive and linguistic practices used by bilingual speakers" (ibid: 325).[12]

In the course of coding my data, the most intricate process was finding the right language to convey the participants' words most adequately. By adopting the participants' practice of translanguaging, I labeled each code I created in the language that carries the meaning of the articulated concept most fittingly. This means, I integrated the practice of translaguaging into the very process of coding my data. Following this approach, my coding list ultimately consisted of German, Turkish and English labels.

Although shifting between Turkish and German abounded in the group discussions I conducted, I did not attempt to describe this in terms of a linguistic analysis. Neither did I approach my bilingual data as combination or mixture of two different languages but rather as heteroglossic assemblages produced within a particular situation. The most intriguing point of this linguo-social product is its quality of 'non-emblematic nature' in terms of its linguistic quality. To avoid creating a universally valid conception of a bilingual space by looking for a meta grammar, what Wei calls "moment analysis" requires attention to the situatedness and intra-citationality of the produced text (Wei 2011; 2013). The aim of such mode of interpretation is to draw attention to the moment or to the situation in which the bilingual text emerges.

---

12 In their article "(Re)conceptualizing Language Advocacy," Ellen Demas and Cinthya M. Saavedra bring to attention that the concept of bilingualism is itself a construct produced through a normative lens of monolinguality, through which being bilingual is constructed "as a true, universal category," which "creates a power position for experts, monolinguals, that allows for the constant control and regulation of those deemed bilingual" (Demas/Saavedra 2004: 221). In fact, a major problem in understanding bilingualism is that it tends to be seen as a side-by-side linear acquisition of two languages, which are both supposedly acquired in similar degrees of proficiency (ibid: 220).

While being German 'native speakers', for the majority of the participants, Turkish represented a secondary language with a limited, often rudimentary range of vocabulary. However, rather than hampering the flow of communication, this mutual linguistic limit (my limited German and their limited Turkish) led to a productively negotiated mode of communication. On the one hand, by giving primacy to Turkish, the group members considered my language constraint.[13] On the other, I encouraged them to speak German as soon as they seemed to encounter difficulties to articulate themselves in Turkish. The negotiated space resulting from the potential productivity of our mutual linguistic constraints evokes Li Wei's concept of "translanguaging space" which is the situated product of "multilingual practices" and multiple "identity positions" constructed through creative and critical use of the linguistic repertoire available (Wei 2011: 1222). In this negotiated space, the language use formed the medium in which the cultural in-betweenness present at the group discussions was most playfully enacted. That is to say, recurring linguistic stumbling blocks were not mere obstacles, but challenges generating a bilingual dimension of my collected data.

By foregrounding criticality, Wei departs from the bulk of research on bi- and multilinguality which tends to put creativity into sharp focus and leaves criticality largely underexplored (cf. Bhatia/Ritchie 2013; Heller 2007; Auer 2002b; Kallmeyer/Keim 2003; Dirim/Hieronymus 2003). According to Wei, criticality is "the ability to use available evidence appropriately, systematically and insightfully [...] to question and problematize received wisdom" (Wei 2011: 1223). However, while in Wei's study creativity and criticality are expressed through "fun" (both in having fun and in making fun of), in my study, they are rather articulated through a certain tension, that is, a sense of unease in relation to the existing set of vocabulary. In my

---

13 For instance, at times they translated their sentences or the words to me, especially when they sensed that it might be too complex for me to understand what they had just discussed.

group discussions, the participants often expressed frustration and dissatisfaction with immediately available expressions. They were highly cognizant of—and often expressed an urge to revise—their choice of words. This is why in a bilingual research setting translation becomes a challenging methodological step in which it is crucial to keep the participants' criticality and creativity alive.

In-Vivo Coding—Living in Translation

Translation has a colonialist charge. Since it has been a primary vehicle in the creation of asymmetric positions between the West and 'the Rest,' translation requires particular sensitivity in a research setting that engages with the vocabulary of cultural difference. Operating under the name of intelligibility, translation always bears the risk of reordering meanings, which threatens to be a reductive adaptation, a simplification of the source language(s) so that the meaning fits into the value grid of the target language. This is not to say that translation can or has to be disposed of altogether. On the contrary, translation can also be productive when it aims at foregrounding the excess of meaning and each language's unintelligible remainders. The task is to resist the urge to streamline meaning for the sake of directness. Or, in other words, rather than to seek a sudden moment of recognition in which all contradictions are resolved, translation's challenge is to create a space in which the very process of making sense comes to the fore. Instead of finding a way to "enjoy the pleasure of the instant," this latter form of translation embraces the delay and deferral of the meaning at play and therefore disrupts the "lazy reason" that "underlies the hegemonic knowledge [...] produced in the West" (de Sousa Santos 2004: 162).[14] In this sense, "the word translation itself

---

14 Drawing on Lebniz, De Sousa Santos describes lazy reason as the lack of effort to go beyond pre-existing models of thinking. Accordingly, lazy reasoning presupposes that it has already found a universal cause-and-effect formula. See: De Sousa Santos 2004.

loses its literal sense, it becomes a catachresis" (Spivak 2000: 13). And in such form, translation can contribute to the project of decolonizing methodology. For this, however, it needs to be understood as a process of interplay between cultural differences, as a transcultural process, working through politics of untranslatability. Or, as Gutiérrez Rodríguez puts it, "[t]he translation project that emerges from transcultural encounters does not pursue the goal of articulating a universal commonality but rather attempts to find a language in 'différence', a language that departs from the 'very possibility of difference" (Gutiérrez Rodríguez 2010: 25).

In a multilingual research setting, using "the English language as the language of research" can be risky when the meaning established is "represented without regard to what is lost in translation and transculturation" (Swadener/Mutua 2004: 258). Although English has become somewhat of a scholarly necessity, as a globally shared language that eases the communication between researchers across different academic contexts and settings, one has to be aware of the fact that it carries with it an imperial past/present. Despite these risks, I see the use of English in my study as a productive diffusion, since it provided a linguistic third, through which neither of the two languages of the empirical setting was privileged. It also facilitated for me the construction of a certain distance and moments of detachment through which the source material could be approached anew.

Yet it is important to note that this study is to a large extent based on an effort of presenting the linguistic complexity of the data. Especially two methodological strategies of Grounded Theory—in-vivo coding and sensitizing concept—proved immensely helpful for unsettling the semblance of monolinguality and avoiding an uncritical imposition of a third, scholarly language. By engaging in translating my data transculturally, my aim was to emphasize the ungraspable remainders of translation, and give the reader a sense of the situatedness of meaning produced by the participants.[15] The concepts produced through in-vivo coding aim at disrupting the appearance of monologuality. The transcultural translation of these concepts responds to the risk of monolingual perception, that is, the risk that, despite their visual difference, these concepts are read through a monolingual lens.[16]

Rather than creating rigidly defined descriptions, sensitizing concepts involves keeping terms open and permeable to the passage of meaning through them in different contexts. "[W]hereas definitive concepts provide prescriptions of what to see," Herbert Blumer writes, "sensitizing concepts merely suggest directions along which to look" (Blumer 1969: 148). In-vivo coding, which means coding "that which is alive," on the other hand, makes it possible to keep the participants' words in the form they were used (Saldaña 2009: 74). In-vivo coding not only "prioritizes and honors the participant's voice" but it also signals the "characteristic of [the] social worlds" articulated (ibid: 74; Charmaz 2006: 56). As Charmaz notes, in-vivo codes can be "general terms everyone 'knows' that flag condensed but significant meanings" or, for instance, "a participant's innovative term that captures meanings or experience," or they can be "insider shorthand terms specific to a particular group that reflect their perspective" (Charmaz 2006: 55).

An example for both in-vivo coding and sensitizing concepts from my study is the participants' use of the Turkish word özenti. Since the meaning of özenti was ambivalent in participants' use, and therefore remains untranslatable, a transcultural translation became

---

15 However, lost in the translation process were the participants' regional Turkish accents and, in many cases, their unconventional use of grammar.

16 A similar strategy is creatively used in Elisabeth Tuider's works "Transnationales Erzählen. Zum Umgang mit Über-setzungen in der Biografieforschung" (2009) and "'Sitting at a Crossroads' Methodisch Einholen: Intersektionalität in der Perspektive der Biographieforschung" (2011).

necessary. A literal translation—which would be wannabe in English or Möchtegern in German—would miss the culturally-specific signification of the word as it was used by the participants in the course of the discussions.[17] By using in-vivo coding, I therefore kept the participants' voice in the original when they used this term. Yet, I also sensitized the concept by emphasizing the ambiguous meaning it created. Tracing the historical and cultural meaning it carries, I explore and highlight the critical tone it conveys regarding notions of modernity and westernization. As an in-vivo code, özenti becomes a term whose meaning is "always already living in translation" (Niranjana 1992: 6).

Another example presents the ambiguous interplay between the German word sittenwidrig and the Turkish word ahlak dışı. If literally translated to English, both words mean 'indecent.' Yet again, such translation would ignore the participants' choice of words. In order to portray the nuanced entanglement of the two words in the discussion, I conceptualize the relation between them as connoting almost the same but not quite. In this case, produced through in-vivo coding, the meaning of these words through a transcultural translation expresses "the central reciprocal relationship between languages" (Benjamin 1969: 72).

In fact, non-verbal articulation such as gestures, postures, and facial expressions can be also subject to coding and even to transcultural translation. For instance, in one of my group discussions, one participant, whose grandparents come from the Western part of Turkey, commented on Lady Bitch Ray's music video with a disparaging ref-

---

17 In a similar fashion, touching upon the risky dimension of the translation, in their article on Edith Enzenhofer and Katharina Resch ask: "can the meaning of the Turkish concept 'namus' be mediated through the German concept 'Ehre' [honor] in a way that we understand what the speaker means?" (Enzenhofer/Resch 2011: para. 66). According to Enzenhofer and Resch "the translator finds herself/himself in ideological question of general translatability and general untranslatability of the text" (ibid: para. 71).

erence to the Eastern part of Turkey. Upon this, two other participants' whose grandparents come from the Eastern part of Turkey exchanged a glance expressing a sense of irritation. Noticing this, the speaker revised and mitigated her statement. Without translating the non-verbal expressions of this scene, the cultural diversity—and the resulting tensions and interactions that were never directly addressed—within the group, would have been lost. My transcultural translation of such gestures thus aims at revealing the fact that sometimes, when one is waiting for the manifestation of meaning in language, it is "enough to notice that the other has already silently made that effort" (Spivak 2000: 22).

SITUATING THE GROUP DISCUSSIONS

The size of the groups varied between 5–6 participants. Group A consisted of female students: Ceren, Jale, Yildiz, Nisa, Yaprak, Funda.[18] Since one participant (Ceren) stated her preference to speak German, this group's session was bilingual from the outset.[19] Group B was a preexisting group made up of five female and one male student—Eda, Esin, Selin, Zeynep, Mehtap, and Berk—all friends who knew each other from the university. Group C was composed of five female participants: Demet, Nurcan, Havva, Leyla, and Serap. What distinguishes this group discussion from the other two is a certain

---

18 All names are used in this study are pseudonyms.
19 Although in the other two groups the participants used fewer German expressions in comparison to Group A, the translation of these group discussions were more challenging for me because of the participants' unconventional grammar use. Peter Auer underlines this challenge by stating that, the moment of language crossing is difficult to capture since they are "grammatical units in which elements from two different languages are conjoined by ambivalent elements which can be part of both" (Auer 2007: 324).

reticence, as it showed twenty-five silent moments, ranging between 5 and 15 seconds.

At the beginning of each group discussion, I asked the participants to fill out a short questionnaire, which included questions concerning their age, birthplace, country of citizenship, university department, languages they speak and their political, social and religious affiliation. I also asked them to provide more information about their family members, their parents' occupation and who of their family members first immigrated to Germany. These questions helped me to get an idea of the diversity of the groups, since they added further details about the group members' individual backgrounds, which in some cases nuanced my analysis.[20]

The participants' age varied between twenty and twenty-five. They were all born and raised in Germany. Five discussants held Turkish passports, one participant held a binational passport, and one participant indicated that she holds a Turkish passport but applied for German citizenship. They studied in departments ranging from sociology, psychology, pedagogy, engineering, and computer science. All participants could speak at least one foreign language such as English, Spanish, and French.[21] Some also indicated that they speak Zazaca and Lazca besides German and Turkish in their daily life.[22] Only one participant rated her Turkish at an excellent level, and only one participant assessed her Turkish skill as insufficient (too elementary for the discussion). All other participants rated their Turkish as

---

20 Filling in the questionnaire was optional. The participants also were notified that they did not have to answer all questions. Moreover, each multiple-choice question included an empty slot in which the participants could fill in alternative answers.
21 Three participants stated that they can speak some of these languages as good as/ or better than Turkish.
22 Zazaca and Lazca are unofficial languages spoken in Turkey. Zazaca is common between Turkish and Kurdish Alevis. Lazca is widely used in the northern part of Turkey.

intermediate or upper intermediate. Except for one participant, whose parents were teachers in a high school, all their parents were employed either as heavy industry laborers or as service sector laborers. The participants' grandparents immigrated to Germany from various cities such as Sivas, Tunceli, Yozgat, Rize, Malatya.[23][24] The forms of political affiliation indicated by the participants were also highly diverse. Whereas six participants indicated that they do not support any political party (neither in Turkey nor in Germany), other participants referred to their political backgrounds as leftist, social democratic, right wing, liberal, socialist, religious, and socialist and religious.[25]

After the participants completed the questionnaire, I asked them to watch twice Lady Bitch Ray's music video "Du Bist Krank." In each group, the participants initially refused to watch the music video again after seeing it for the first time.[26] I kicked off the discussion by asking 'What is your first impression about her? What do you think about the video?'

---

[23] Some participants answered this question by writing Turkey rather than naming any specific city.

[24] These cities are all located in different regions of Turkey. This diversity is also reflected by the participants' differing Turkish accents. Since a larger analysis of these linguistic differences exceeds the scope of this project, I highlight this fact to inform the reader about the diversity within the groups.

[25] Without choosing any political label given in the questionare, two participants ticked off the Green Party and the Left Party as the parties they vote for.

[26] Interestingly, however, approximately an hour into the discussion, they themselves asked to rewatch it.

Informant Participants—the Knowledge that is (not) Power

In each group, I introduced my project to the participants and provided introductory information about Lady Bitch Ray before starting the music video. However, naturally, I did not have total control over the amount of information available to the group. In each group, at least one member knew Lady Bitch Ray, and in the course of the discussions, these informant participants shared their knowledge with the other members: in Group A Ceren and Funda, in Group B Zeynep, in Group C Serap.

The informant participants each time increased their interaction. Each time the informant participants' providing of further information did each time increase the level of interaction. When no additional details were given, the discussions developed into arrays of speculative statements marked by phrases like 'perhaps', 'it seems like', and 'may be'. However, being positioned as knowledgeable about Lady Bitch Ray, at times, created moments of discomfort for the informant participants. After being directly or indirectly questioned regarding their awareness of LBR, in all three groups the informant participants began to justify their interest. For instance, in Group B, after a sarcastic comment by Berk, Zeynep downplayed the reasons for the extent of her knowledge:

Extract 1

(Selin): She's pretty famous already. She was also in Harald Schmidt's [TV] show.

(Zeynep): Right.

(Selin): And she also had *a show* on Viva.

(Zeynep): Yes, and she worked as a radio host.

(Selin): Yes, she had a show, which she hosted weekly. From a bed.

(Zeynep): Right.

(Berk): You're seriously hooked! /Laughter/

(Berk): cool [ironic/sarcastic].

(Zeynep): Well, when I see something Turkish and *extrovert*, I'm quite hooked: who is that? Where does she come from? What's happening?

In a similar situation, another informant participant, Funda (Group A) also tried to explain why she knows LBR.

Extract 2

(Funda): Well, as a curious aunt [merakli Melahat, Turkish proverb] Funda, I wanted to at least once look at it and then when I saw it, I said "Hmm, what is this?"

(Yaprak): Have you regretted it?

(Funda): No, I just watched, and I watched everything I could. I read…and then ask myself why this girl behaves like that. **Just wanted to know.** And then…[laughs]… whatever…in the end, it was just too much!

In fact, after being questioned, they made not only attempts at justifying their knowledge but made also statements in which they distanced themselves from LBR.

Extract 3

(Zeynep): I just want to tell you that there are various types of pro..pro..*provocation*. I found her [LBR] also really extreme. I don't want to be misunderstood!
(All together): Whatever you say [tabi tabi]! [laughs].

Similarly, in Group A, after disagreeing with her co-participants' wholesale condemnation of LBR, Ceren disassociated herself from LBR by saying "I wouldn't do this myself either." And she further explains, "Well, I mean, this is just her style. She has her own style...OK, I wouldn't be into this either and...well, say "wow, what a great clip."

In fact, that some participants knew LBR, on the one hand, stimulated, and on the other hand, stalled the discussion. Since the informants often found themselves in the position of having to legitimize their knowledge, in each session, they, at times, also just remained silent as if withholding information they could have provided. These moments of silence were particularly frequent in Group C, a point I discuss in detail in the following part.

The Unsaid in the Said; The Said in the Unsaid—Digressions and Silences

Undervalued and often seen as an error, "silence is frequently overlooked in qualitative research" (Poland/Pederson 1998: 293). Written out of the findings, silence is often discarded as a failure in the search for meaning. Or, when it is included, it is often just reduced as cultural specific attitudes. However, as I maintain in this study, silence is meaningful with respect to the condition it is generated in the research setting. It has to be seen not merely as a part of but, in fact, as a productive element in the data, often precisely because of its apparent articulation of unproductivity. According to Poland and Pederson, far from indicating passivity, moments of silence are "actively chosen" and therefore can also be seen as interventions in the conversation flow (Poland/Pederson 1998: 300). Instead of leaving a gap in the transmission of meaning, silence, in this sense, is the moment of deceleration, a moment in which meaning accumulates and intensifies. Adele Clarke calls these moments of intensity "sites of silence" (Clarke 2005: 85). Silence is situated. In his introduction to Silence: Interdisciplinary Perspectives, Adam Jaworski underscores the importance of taking into account the context of silence's events (Jaworski 1997: 3). Accordingly, silence may mean "withholding or resistance, or it may reflect a cultural mode of self-representation; it may reflect what is taken for granted or what goes without saying, or it may represent that which cannot be said, the unthinkable" (Poland/Pederson 1998: 294; my emphasis).

In Group C, I recorded twenty-one silent moments of various lengths between five to fifteen seconds. It is difficult to give exact reasons as for why these moments occurred in this group particularly. One reason might however be that Group C's informant participant (Serap) provided less information compared to the informants in Group A and Group B. Another reason might be that pivotal information—such as LBR's Turkish cultural background and her academic career—was revealed relatively late in Group C. Moreover, reticence might have functioned as resistance. In this sense, the silent moments represented a form of protest against the binary opposition of either approving or disapproving LBR's performance. This would mean that the participants refused to fix their positions into a pre-established grid of being 'conservative' or even 'backward' on the one hand, and being 'tolerant' or 'open minded' on the other.[27] In this respect, the frequent pauses in Group C's discussion can be read as an example of the fact that "silence is not the lack of talk but it is the ap-

---

27 I elaborate on this point in chapter 3 with respect to how the participants avoided certain discursive traps by not using certain terms, by reformulating their expressions or just keeping silent.

propriate amount and type of talk in particular context" (Sifinau 1997: 55).

If silence can be charged with meaning, voice can withhold and defer it. Speech can also create a site of silence, even accentuate silence. That Group C's participants remained relatively more reticent does not mean that they were less involved than the other groups' participants were. For instance, in Group A, it was hard to sustain the participants' focus on the topic, as they frequently digressed and diverted from the topic. I termed these thematic ruptures in the talk as digressionary moments—moments that disrupt the topic but not the ongoing flow of the discussion. Through this term, I attempt to highlight the centrality of the act of evading and diverting. Far from being 'only' asides or adjuncts in the argumentative flow, these moments were crucial (functionally speaking), precisely because they offered a welcomed relieve from the tension produced by the topic. Furthermore, keeping the discussion vivid by sustaining interaction, the participants resorted to sudden digressions in order to counteract exhaustion of the topic and to avoid silence.

In the course of Group A's discussion, I coded six digressionary moments whose topics were ranging from more or less random issues such as wearing braces to the difference between the words 'Muslim' and 'Islamist' and a discussion on having or not having a Facebook account. With this in mind, I interpret the use of digressions in Group A as a "conversational tool or strategic device which is used to overcome silences" (Poland/Pederson 1998: 299). The digressions occurred "for the sake of avoiding socially awkward silences or to purposely conceal information, in which case, it may be seen as containing a certain emptiness or silence of its own" (ibid: 299).

The refusal to speak in Group C and the digressionary moments in Group A show how *voice can include silence* and *silence can include voice*. Since silence does not merely indicate passivity, the lack of interaction in Group C cannot be reduced to disengagement only. In fact, as Maria Sifianou remarks, the very sign of disengagement might indicate "a deep bond between interactants," as it can communicate "shared mutual knowledge [...] with very little or no verbalization" (Sifianou 1997: 78). In this sense, silence can signal "high involvement" (Scollon/Scollon 2012: 50). Similarly, increased interaction does not mean absolute engagement. The digressionary moments showed how words might be employed *against* the production of meaning or against the immediately available modes of producing meaning.

THE PROJECT MAP: A TREFOIL KNOT

After creating the categories (the main topics debated) I developed my maps to illustrate the argumentative and positional themes salient in the group discussions. In line with my interpretation of the occurred silences and digressionary moments, these maps do not only visualize the present, articulated themes, but also those, which remained tacit, obscured, evaded, unarticulated. I focused therefore not only on what was explicit in my data, but also on the gaps and absences that emerged between the prominent narratives.

The triangular shape of my social arenas map (Fig. 1) emerged because of the prominence of three major topics—Feminism, Germanness, Turkishness. Important to note is here that, while I consider these terms as methodologically productive, I nevertheless see them as situated in the empirical context in which they emerged. In other words, they do not reflect my own conceptualization or perspective on the issues discussed, but took shape from the participants' own words. As Floya Anthias warns us, it is important to keep in mind that "[s]ubjects [...] often use essentialized versions of identity of which their researchers are skeptical. We must ask what does the actual concept, for analytical purposes, enable or alternatively what does it disable" (Anthias 2002: 492). Thus, in order to subvert the reproduction of essentializing terms, it is not enough to merely avoid these terms or replace them by deconstructionist concepts, as the question remains how exactly these problematic terms are used in actual practice. The real challenge consists therefore in mapping out the situated relations that mark the formation of such essentializing categories. This means, rather than reaffirming the categories in question, my maps aim at visualizing the interplay and entanglements that bring these categories into being, showing how "different categories are formed and reformed through one another" (Barad 2001: 99).

In this sense, this social arenas map (Fig. 1) shows the participants' constantly changing and often contradictory modes of positioning. In other words, it depicts the participants' footsteps, their movement in their interpretation of Lady Bitch Ray's performance, depicted by the lines inside the diagram, which outline the paths that linked the main topics to one other.

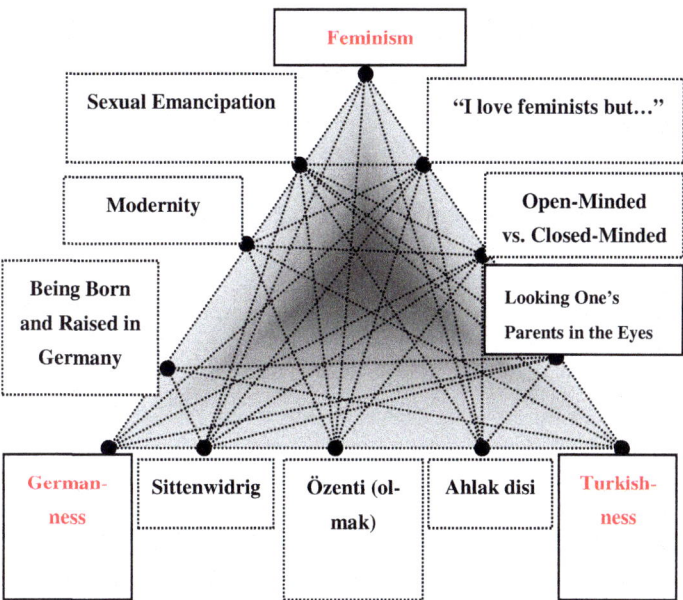

Figure 1: Social Arenas Map—Two-Dimensional Knot.

I developed my project map (Fig. 2) by creating an abstract image of the social arenas map (Fig 1). Rather than displaying the most immediately available categories, this map aims to convey the movement in between the discourses. It shows how the seemingly intersecting paths shown on the social arenas map are entangled with one another in a complex assemblage. The trefoil knot (Fig. 2) represents the dynamic form of positioning, including the gaps, silences, evasions, digressions, and discursive turns. Although I consider this image as more adequately conveying the spirit of my empirical research, I still find it important to show the two dimensional version (Fig. 1) in order to visualize the topics that conditioned the knotty entanglements.

Figure 2: Project Map—Three-Dimensional (Trefoil) Knot.

The trefoil knot therefore depicts the movement that marks the inner space of the triangle of my social arenas map. It animates the dynamic movements of the participants within and across discourses. It maps out the trajectories of the empirical "field as a set of discourses, a field where dialogues are created, entered, left, and revisited on many occasions and in many different forms" (Lincoln/Denzin 2003: 9). By tracing the participants' discursive routes, in the following chapter, I present their dynamic positioning with regard to what I conceptualize as a transcultural locational feminist perspective.

Not Yet A Code—Transcultural Locational Feminism

In this chapter, I present the predominant themes that emerged with the positional maps and social arenas maps drawn from my group discussions. These maps reveal that the participants were not only shifting incoherently between discourses such as national identity and popular culture, but that they were also holding multiple positions at the same time. As I argue, their movements between positionalities of Turkishness, Germanness and Feminism reveal rhetorical gaps in which the potential to think feminism otherwise, that is, the potential for a not-yet existing discourse of transcultural locational feminism(s), emerges.

TURKISHNESS, OR WHERE ON EARTH?

In each group, family represented a predominant theme through which the participants (dis)located and reconceptualized notions of 'Turkishness' in relation to morality, education, ethnicity and religion. These, what can be called, positional turns were most pronounced in their attempts at framing LBR's cultural (non)belonging.

"Looking one's Parents in the Eyes"

Trying to make sense of LBR's performance, the participants first embarked on biographical investigations, debating with intense curiosity LBR's family background and upbringing. Rather than focusing on her performance as such, they situated her in personal narratives, looking for potential causes that might have produced her 'deviant', 'excessively vulgar' mode of articulation. At an early stage of the discussions, the family was singled out as the original milieu where it must have happened. Asking the informant participants and me for additional background information, the discussants created speculative stories—with numerous 'maybes' and 'perpahses'—about LBR's personal history. Since I remained relatively silent (because of the interesting speculations and fictional pasts created) and since the informant participants were either hesitant to reveal further information in order to avoid being associated with LBR (or simply due to the rudimentary form of their knowledge) the participants used the biographical snippets provided and embellished these with cause-and-effect assumptions. Their knowledge remained limited to the fact that LBR's family came to Germany as guest workers from Sivas—a small city in Central Anatolia—a fact that, as I will show later in this chapter, produced locationally specific narratives with respect to what counts as 'Turkish' and what not.

As a response to my opening question concerning their first impressions of the music video, Jale, a member of Group A, said with astonishment, "[h]er family...the first thing I thought about." As if continuing the sentence and giving voice to Jale's concerns, Funda exclaimed dramatically "What happened? What did they do wrong? Why did this happen?" Although they knew very little about them, almost all participants showed intense sympathy for LBR's parents. Slipping into the shoes of these fictional parents, the participants reenacted and re-felt the family's emotional response to the music video of their daughter. In fact, their scenarios framed her family's reaction in ready-made, ethno-culturally typecasting images of Turkishness. That is, they instantly resorted to a sense of shock, shame and disgrace: "How can she still look in their eyes?"; "Presumably they disinherited her"; "Maybe they are even dead"; "Maybe they don't know anything about this." "They have seen this, for sure," Jale remarked, "but with what kind of feelings?"

Veering away from their emotional alignment with the imagined parents, they then assumed a more distant, observant, third position by highlighting that the reason for LBR's 'moral transgression' must be found in a malfunctioning parent-child relation, if not in downright parental failure. Thus, they argued that LBR's exaggerated, 'abnormal' acting is an indicator of 'ineffective' parental control, that is, a disciplinary maladjustment of either being too slack or too coercive. In this positional turn, therefore, the family and its pedagogical practices were isolated as being fully responsible for the child's attitude towards societal morals, especially when it comes to issues of gender, intimacy, and sexuality.

After discussing how these kinds of music videos are detrimental to the 'personality development' of adolescents, especially that of young girls, Group B highlighted the importance of parental monitoring particularly during puberty.

Extract 1

(Selin): If the family is there [for her] and if they have a proper relationship, the girl manages to get over this phase, that is, *puberty*[1].
(Eda): Yes, I think so, too. If the family brings her up properly, the girl thinks, "I was brought up in certain way"...
(Esin): You keep on harping on the family too much. What does it have to do with the family?
(Selin): Yes, of course! The family is important! Very important!
(Zeynep): I would like to say one more thing...

---

1 Italics in the extracts indicate words spoken in German.

(Eda): I also think that the family is most important.

(Zeynep): The family...but listen, every kid, who experiences *puberty* goes through such things. For some it's tough. For others it's not that tough.
(Eda): Yes, of course!
(Zeynep): It can be red lipstick, but it can also be something completely else! It can be anything. For some it's only lipstick, for others curly hair and lipstick and *high heels*. Well... high heels. Everybody has something, and that's normal. And then it ends. One time or another, it'll be over, too!
(Selin): But for some not! For some it doesn't end, but it goes on and on and even gets worse. For instance, we all got over our *puberty*. All of us have been in *puberty*. We all have dirty laundry somewhere.
/Laughs/
(Berk): Really? [smiling]
(Selin): Yes. But what's important...we didn't go that far...that's important, how far one goes. Um...I...um...first comes the family...um...my mother...um...my father...um, well, um...I always live my life in a way that I can still look my parents in the eyes. Well, um...how should I explain that?
(Zeynep): Without mistakes?
(Selin): Of course, everybody makes mistakes! But not such a big mistake! If I'd make such a big mistake, how could I still look my father in the eye?

In this extract, a central opposition develops between Selin and Zeynep. Selin argues that parental guidance is necessary to avoid that the 'symptoms' of puberty establish themselves as 'chronic', essential personal traits. On the other hand, seemingly encouraged by Esin's admonishing remark that Selin keeps on "harping on the family,"

Zeynep claims that one should see adolescent disobedience as temporal and "normal."

The example of red lipstick and high heels in Zeynep's statement is remarkable here. In reference to sexuality and puberty, this example is of course not randomly chosen. On the contrary, it stands for the 'bitchy' appearance associated with sexual explicitness. It is important to underline the fact that the image of red lipstick and high heels was first brought to the table by Berk (the only male participant of all conducted group discussions) who complained about the 'degeneration' of Turkish-German kids, who, in his words, "live in Turkish ghettos." In his early remarks, Berk expressed his discomfort with the fact that, in 'Turkish' neighborhoods, girls begin to wear high heels and apply red lipstick at an 'intolerably' early age. Indirectly referring to (and thereby contradicting) Berk's view, Zeynep does not see such transgressions concerning shifts in the construction of one's image as a necessarily alarming fact. She describes puberty as an exploratory phase—"everybody has something." For her, during puberty, 'womanhood' as such is subject to various makeovers as part of an inevitable process of coming of age. "One time or another," she maintains, "it'll be over."

Despite the fact that Selin doubts this, she tones down her voice and says, "We all have dirty laundry somewhere." Yet, in her view, there are certain kinds of transgressions that are unforgivable. The border of 'how far one can go', or, in other words, 'how dirty the laundry can get', is demarcated by the criteria of whether one can still 'look one's parents in the eyes.' This formulation evokes Sue Lees' conceptualization of 'reputation' among adolescent girls. In her Losing out: Sexuality and Adolescent Girl, Lees explores the experience of female teenagers in British schools by examining how particular acts such as "having a steady boyfriend" or "sleeping around with random boys" serve as markers of "guarding" or "loosing" status (Lees 1986: 38). Lees' conceptualization helps to understand the role of sexuality in strategies of self-representation of adolescents, not only in schools but also in other social environments, including the family. Yet, as Avtar Brah has shown in her Cartographies of Diaspora, these seemingly universal value-categories are way less clear-cut, since they have their culturally specific modalities. Analyzing Lees' account, Brah underlines the situatedness of the very concept of 'reputation'. "[W]hen applied to Asian girls [in Britain]", Brah states, "having a boyfriend would in itself constitute a transgression from certain norms of 'respectability'" (Brah 1996: 78). In other words, the boundary of transgression is determined by locationally inflected ethico-sexual ideals.

Referring to the issue of 'having a boyfriend' for 'Turkish families in Germany', Nurcan (Group C) develops a perspective that problematizes parental repressive control. As she sees it, parent-child relations should ideally be based on mutual empathy.

Extract 2

(Nurcan): For instance, let's say, a girl is in love with someone. And she tells her mother. If her mother says, "of course, you have a heart, too. But you should be careful about this and that" Instead of saying that...if she says "Do you want to disgrace us? I'll tell your father." And then, the father comes and says "I've heard you're seeing someone! You better get married!"...Now, who wouldn't hate this culture? Parents have to understand their own culture and religion better.

(Demet): Yes, absolutely! It's because of ignorance [bilincsizlik], which causes these kinds of problems.

(Nurcan): Then she goes to school. One says "I have a *boyfriend*! What about you?" She replies, "No, I don't! It's forbidden for me. I'm a Turk." Actually, she could have explained it differently, had her parents treated her differently.

/Silence/

(Nurcan): For instance, what is considered as wrong for girls should be also considered wrong for boys. Here, Turkish families are proud of saying "our son has a boyfriend [sic]" But are they proud when their daughter does the same thing? No, they aren't.

(?): Yes.
(?): Right.
(Nurcan): Therefore, Germans say, "your boys are very free, they do whatever they want! But for your girls, everything is forbidden." Actually, this kind of behavior is not correct for neither of them...it's shown wrong. In this instance, Turkish culture...Islam comes across as being oppressive. Well, it's not true at all; in fact, it's ignorance [cahillik] that causes oppression.

Told in highly dramatized, theatrical scenes, Nurcan's narrative illustrates her view on 'misinterpretations' of Turkish cultural norms and values. The first scene of her strikingly lively account takes place in a domestic, private space. The protagonist is an adolescent girl who confides to her mom her love for "someone." Set in a forking-path framework, the protagonist faces two possible narrative arcs, determined by different reactions from the mother. In one plotline, we see an idealized mother-daughter relation, depicted through the mother's supportive, yet advisory, response. The other plotline features an unsympathetic mother who, alarmed with a sense of disgrace, threatens to sneak the daughter's secret to the authoritarian father. Then, the father enters the scene. He bursts out harshly (indicated by Nurcan's change of intonation): "I heard you're seeing someone! You better get married!" The scene ends with Nurcan's rhetorical question: "Now, who wouldn't hate this culture?"

Encouraged by Demet's supportive interjection, Nurcan goes on with a second scene, which takes place in a school. Now the protagonist faces a friend's question as to why she does not have a boyfriend. In her response, the protagonist refers to her Turkishness, which is linked up with parental restrictions. As Nurcan concludes, it is precisely this parental misinterpretation of cultural codes that locks

Turkishness into a discursive paradigm of restriction. That is, for her, it is not Turkish culture itself that denies Nurcan's character any sense of agency, but rather it is how 'original' cultural values are adversely applied and practiced. As Nurcan maintains, had the parents treated her "differently" (as she suggested in her alternative plotline) the girl could have explained herself "differently." Interestingly, Nurcan does not give concrete examples of these 'different' explanations and thus expands the realm of possible answers. What this evokes is a potential poly-positionality within the demarcated cultural territory of Turkishness.

Another interesting point of this extract is how Nurcan formulates a version of gender equality. After a brief moment of silence, she complains about the gender-biased pedagogical approach of Turkish parents in Germany. While these parents disapprove of non-marital relationships for their daughters, she explains with agitated gestures, the same parents show a sense of pride when their "sons have boyfriends." In my reading, this striking slip of the tongue stands for the very centrality of gender for the culturally specific parent-child relations at issue. In this respect, it displays the quintessential character of the phrase 'having a boyfriend' for the cultural milieu she portrays.

According to Nurcan, the gender-biased approach to parenting is perceived by Germans as an injustice inherent to Turkish culture, rather than as ignorance on the side of individual parents. In a defamiliarizing manner, however, Nurcan does not approach the issue in the conventional way (with arguments that girls should be able to do anything 'boys can do'), but, with a crucial rhetorical difference, she frames it under consideration of culturally specific values and norms, and gender-equal application of these. In her article Custom Tailored Islam? Second Generational Female Students of Turko-Muslim Origin in Germany, Yasemin Karakaşoğlu conceptualizes a similar statement made by one of her participants as "equality of restrictions"

(Karakaşoğlu 2003: 118).[2] Karakaşoğlu's choice of words remains, however, problematic, since the concept of restriction presupposes an oppositional relation to freedom. Particularly with respect to Nurcan's statement, rather than an "equality of restrictions," this approach should be seen as a call for an equality of requirements in accordance with idealized cultural norms and values.

As the site where Turkish culture is supposedly (re)produced, the participants conceived the family as the site where Turkish culture is also misproduced, dispersed, and transformed. That is to say, while creating an 'original' Turkishness, it was seen also as an interim space that is supposed to reinscribe a transcending cultural ideal. The central question therefore is when exactly, in the participants' views, Turkish culture is properly and when poorly reproduced. This question can be approached by means of inquiries into what Sara Ahmed has called the "cultural politics of emotion" embodied, as I read the participants' arguments, in the affective dynamics of parent-child relations (Ahmed 2004).

These affective dynamics cannot be reduced to notions such as 'emotional pressure'. As Berrin Özlem Otyakmaz shows in her studies, the affective dynamics attached to discourses such as 'having a boyfriend' are not to be understood as oppressive cultural norms (Otyakmaz 1990: 80; 1993: 77). Rather, these discourses are always in the process of being contested and negotiated within affective bonds formed in structures such as the family. In this respect, the family is a particular system of empathy, in which one takes, even claims, positions through attachments and exchanges of emotions. As Ahmed puts it, because they are moving in structures but also themselves structuring, emotions are investments in forms of positioning—they "involve [...] affective forms of reorientation" (Ahmed

---

2 Karakaşoğlu's interviewee says, "I would treat them equally. For instance I wouldn't allow my son or my daughter to go to the discotheque or to have sexual intercourse with the other sex before marriage" (Karakaşoğlu 2003: 118).

2004: 8). In the participants' construction, the family is not just as a space of reinforcement and normativization, but also as a political site in which one empathizes with and against one another vis-à-vis social norms. In other words, the family becomes an affectively contested testing-ground for a hypothetical Turkishness and its idealized criteria. As recurrently articulated in the discussions, 'having a boyfriend' forms a particular discursive field in which one's position towards ideals of Turkishness are enacted through politics of emotion.

This cultural contestation of what is (and can be) intimately felt is played out most forcefully in the realm of gender and sexuality. Representing a rhetorical and social enactment of sexuality, 'having a boyfriend' is implicitly associated with the ability to 'look one's parents in the eyes'. It is interesting to see how in Selin's rhetorical strategy this ability to 'look one's parents in the eyes' subtly transforms into an ability to look one's father in the eyes, which hints at the pronounced gendered dimension of cultural norms and values. Tested in the family are not the requirements per se—since these requirements are bound up with larger cultural ideals of Turkishness—but primarily their application. In order to apply these values equally, Nurcan remarks, "parents should know their own culture better." In the participants' language, gender equality cannot be achieved by way of transgressions of these affectively coded boundaries, since this would mean a violation within the familial system of empathy. That is why the concept of "equality of restriction" should be modified to an equality of requirements. For the discussants, sexual promiscuity does not translate into notions of sexual freedom. The fact of not allowing (from the parental perspective) does not necessarily imply restriction, because the concept of restriction presupposes a predetermined way of transgression. Similarly, the fact of not doing (from the adolescent perspective) does not necessarily mean obedience, an existence in oppression or, in repression. In mere linguistic terms, it is therefore the resort to a framework of negation that produces a notional lack of agency. Nurcan points to this lack when she problematizes the discursive link between not having a boyfriend and Turkishness. The participants' concept of Turkishness does not hinge on, in simple terms, whether one has a boyfriend or whether one has non-marital sex, since practices of not doing are implicated in a convergence between ethics and empathy. In other words, it is not just a question of what is right and what is wrong. It matters how ethics are emotionally structured, enacted and contested. Values and norms of Turkishness are felt as right or wrong by means of affective links, in the mode of what Avtar Brah describes as the "strong emotional and psychological attachment" articulated within a system of "not letting the family down" (Brah 1996: 78). What are assumed to be universally valid characteristics of Turkish norms and values thereby take on shapes and validities through enactments of familial bonds.

In fact, when Zeynep reveals that LBR has full support from her family, this system is displayed as contingent upon how it is interpreted and acted out.

Extract 3

(Zeynep): Yes, I think so, too. But her family stands by her. They're there for her. They support that, too. Her family comes from Sivas..um…and they back her.
/Laughs altogether/

By overemphasizing LBR's familial support, Zeynep challenges Selin's generalizing assumption that LBR made a "great mistake." For Zeynep, the very framework of assessing moral consequences is not fixed and thus not universally applicable. Using Selin's pattern of moral evaluation, she reformulates it as a situated context of ethical practices. If, in Zeynep's interpretation, moral boundaries of Turkishness do only exist by means of their mode of enactment, what counts as immoral and deviant is also not sweepingly generalizable but determined by intersubjectively embedded and negotiated thresholds of transgression. Put simply, Zeynep makes clear that LBR does not let her family down *either*.

Although Zeynep's striking argument seemed provocative and, as I expected, highly stimulating concerning the debate about familial support, interestingly, what caught her coparticipants' immediate attention was her reference to Sivas, a city in middle Anatolia where LBR's parents come from. Presenting the ensuing debate about Sivas, in the following section, I will probe the participants' depiction of a translocally 'rooted' form of Turkishness.

From Duisburg to Istanbul—Transcultural Geographies

The fact that LBR's family comes from Sivas caused a sudden outburst of laughter from the participants in Group A and Group B.

Extract 4

(Jale): Where are they [parents] from?
(M):   From Sivas
/Laughs altogether/
(Jale): Yeah, that location fits well!

Similar to this extract from Group A, the members of Group B reacted with great surprise when they got the background information from Zeynep. In both groups, the laughter was followed by murmurs and sardonic comments that implied obvious evidence for what caused LBR to act in the way she does. As Funda says: "Yeah, that location fits well." What the participants were implicitly referring to, is the conservative image of the city of Sivas, which inscribed itself into cultural memory through what is commonly known as the *Madimak Massacre* in which thirty-six Alevi artists and musicians were burned to death by a group of so-called 'radical Islamists' (Sökefeld 2008: 67–69).[3] This incident left its mark on Sivas' local

---

3   In this unexpected reference, I also encountered my own preconceptions regarding the participants' cultural positionalities. Even though I consid-

history and created a stereotypical image of its residents as 'dinci,' which translates into an amalgam of 'reactionary' and 'religiously fanatical'.

While it is important to take note of this display of transcultural literacy, more striking for me was the participants' way of linking locationally-specific histories with identity construction. They inferred from the fact that LBR's parents come from Sivas that she must have had a very 'conservative' upbringing. Rushing to the conclusion that LBR's family must be 'dinci', her performance suddenly made sense to them, because they conceived it as a rebellious counter-reaction of a hitherto suppressed daughter.

In fact, the linkage between identity and locality is further emphasized when the participants orient the discussion towards Germany (extract below). This time, however, it is not a singular space that is seen as an environment that could have produced LBR's character. Still, if not a singular place, it remained a specific site marked by its working-class connotation.

Extract 5

(Funda): Absolutely! If she [LBR] lives in Duisburg, then it's normal.
(Ceren): Bremen. Well, because she [Funda] now said Duisburg, that's why.
(Funda): Oh, really, I thought it's Duisburg. Okay. Isn't she there anymore...in Duisburg?
(Nisa): Why Duisburg? And why is that normal there? I mean, why did you say that it's normal in Duisburg? What's going on in Duisburg?

---

ered them as belonging to Turkish and German culture at the same time, when it came to cultural memory, I reverted to national boundaries and hence was surprised by their knowledge of such a specific Turkish historical event.

(Funda): Have you ever been to Duisburg?
(Nisa): No.
(Yıldız): I just say *Liveparade*. That was also there.
(Jale): Aha, *Loveparade*.
(Funda): I'd say, in Duisburg, as a girl you cannot go out alone on the streets after 4pm.
(Yıldız): Yes, I've heard that, too.
(Jale): How do you know that?
(Funda): My family lives there.
(Jale): I see.
(Funda): When I want to go there….
(Nisa): But why is it like that?
(Funda): Huh? Ah, because of the Turks. Because of all those men…*pimps, brawl, knife, stabbing, shooting.* My uncle, on my father's side, died there. My uncles on my mother's side…they kill each other there, one after another! *They are sick there!*
(Jale): Hmm…
(Funda): It's really *asozial* there. The Turkish girls there are either extremely veiled [kapalı], I mean with headscarves, or extremely permissive.
(Yıldız): You mean there is no moderate level.
(Funda): No, there is no moderate level.
(Ceren): *No, well I… well…my relatives also live in Duisburg…and I don't see it like that at all.*
(Funda): *Where do they live?*
(Ceren): *In Duisburg.*
(Funda): *But where?*
(Ceren): *Um…I don't know where exactly, in which district. Once my aunt was there…not anymore, though…they are divorced, but I still know that my relatives are there.*
(Funda): *Aha, I see.*
(Ceren): *That's why…*

(Yıldız): Perhaps, it depends on which borough you live in...that one experiences it differently.
(Ceren): *I don't think so!* When you go to *Cologne*...it's even worse there.
(Yıldız): Yes.
(Nisa): But it's everywhere like that. Berlin is also like that. You cannot lump everyone together and then condemn everyone wholesale and say, "it's same everywhere."
(Yaprak): *What about Nordstadt then?*
(Funda): *That's a joke!*
(Nisa): Yes, but that doesn't mean all of Kassel is like that.
(Funda): *Yes, but Kassel, well...Kassel is a joke in comparison to...*I wouldn't compare them. Let's say Istanbul, Taksim...*fits quite well.*
/Laughs/

Funda makes the interesting claim that LBR's behavior can be seen as 'normal' if one considers her social background, "Duisburg." Vocalizing an obvious question, Nisa asks with bewilderment, "Why Duisburg? And why is it normal there?" Funda replies with a rhetorical question: "Have you ever been to Duisburg?" In her portrayal, Duisburg is a notoriously dangerous city whose streets become, for girls, an unsafe territory after dark. According to her, what makes it so dangerous are Turkish men, whose infamous lifestyle is described by her with a string of nouns uttered in one breath—"pimps," "brawl," "knife," "stabbing," "shooting." Summarizing her illustration, she uses the term *asozial*, whose colloquial meaning could be compared to the American slur 'redneck', derogatorily connoting a 'vulgar', distinctively lower class, 'trashy' appearance and 'morally degenerate' social manners (Mörchen 2011: 88). For Funda, LBR's performance evokes an entire social milieu marked with notions of deviance and abnormality. In an environment where, as she puts it, everybody is "sick," LBR's behavior is just 'normal'.[4]

Hence, as if describing a parallax effect, where the object's position is relative to the subject's gaze, Funda's comment renders one's moral outlook as locationally dependent. While she typecasts Duisburg's male residents as violent criminals, she describes women growing up in this morally deviant milieu as "either extremely religious or extremely permissive." Because Ceren contradicts this description, the discussants detach the characteristics of Funda's Duisburg and define them as belonging not to a specific city, but to a social area, a socio-cultural locale that transcends geographical boundaries, a marginal space, a 'notorious borough', or, as Berk calls it, a "ghetto".[5]

---

4   Since the participants do not name a specific neighborhood, I can only assume that they are referring to Duisburg Marxloh. In Patricia Ehrkamp's article "'I've had it with them!' Younger Migrant Women's Spatial Practices of Conformity and Resistance," an interviewee who is a resident in Marxloh, makes a similar claim that supports my assumption. Ehrkamp participant's, Zehra, says: "Marxloh is a typical macho neighborhood. From 6pm on girls aren't allowed on the street anymore...Turkish women and German women are afraid to go outside by themselves..." (Ehrkamp 2013: 29). In media reports, Marxloh is often cast as the stereotypical 'German ghetto'. A short documentary entitled "Duisburg-Marxloh: Ghetto oder Integration" repeatedly emphasizes the 'invasion of German streets' by Turks, which turns the question as to who represents the ethnic minority upside down. Responding to the interviewer's notably biased question concerning the ethno-cultural composition in Marxloh, an elderly woman says sardonically, "also, Sagen wir so: integrieren müssen wir uns hier!" [Well, let's put it that way: It is we who have to integrate themselves here] (Duisburg-Marxloh: Ghetto oder Integration 2010: min. 00:16:40).

5   According to Maria Stehle, "the politics of ghetto representation" in Germany changed "from the mid-1990s to the twenty-first century"

Bringing in a local example for the marginal space they are trying to define, Yaprak suggests Kassel Nordstadt. However, Funda disagrees by saying that, in comparison to Duisburg, Nordstadt is "a joke" because it corresponds only in principle but not in its extent or in its intensity to what she means. Ridiculing Nordstadt, and in order to capture the social intensity she finds in Duisburg, Funda refers to the Taksim Square in Istanbul. With this, however, the marginal space as such looses its characteristics of marginality and moves to the center. Put differently, it is rhetorically gentrified and becomes a mythically charged, touristic space, where one consumes the phantasmagoric pressures of social congestion and the urban spectacle of what is imagined as 'street life'. Moreover, Funda's reference to Taksim Square operates not only as this deconstruction of the 'ghetto', but it also signals a mode of thinking that inhabits in transcultural geography.

If Kassel Nordstadt is held up to ridicule in Group A, in Group B it is assigned an authentic ghetto-like image. In contrast to Funda, who always remained only a visitor to the Duisburg she describes, Berk positions himself as originally coming from Kassel Nordstadt, which he describes as "a sort of ghetto," a "milieu," whose "conditions are really not nice". It is this milieu, where, according to Berk, Turkish girls become "sluts" ((line 662)). LBR is for him a prime example for the "Turkish girls" (in his ex-neighborhood, Nordstadt) who "at the age of 13" start to wear "tons of makeup" ((lines 154:156)).

(Stehle 2012: 4). The meaning of 'ghetto' lost its post-WWII connotation of segregated Jewish neighborhoods and acquired an 'alarming' sense of similarity between so-called immigrant residencies emerging in Germany and the predominantly Black and Hispanic neighborhoods in the US (2012: 13). Nowadays, Stehle writes, in the German context ghettos stand for "potential traps that confine the Other to certain space and role," and, at the same time, for paradoxical locations that bring forth "notions of spatial multiplicity" (2012: 5).

Though repeatedly complaining about a supposed moral degeneration of Turkish-German girls, for Berk, girls in Turkey do also not truly represent what he assumes to be original Turkish values. In the following extract, he tells an anecdote about his female cousin visiting him from Izmir.

Extract 6

(Berk): They came here. They dress very strangely. The whole makeup and so on that scares me already /laughs/ Well, that *painted face* and those clothes. So, then we went out. We went to the city. Then I told her "just walk ten meters away from me." Well, we went to the city, you know. Then she saw that place and they said immediately, *"Klein-Istanbul."* Turks everywhere! The mother wears a headscarf, carries a baby, has a buggy and walks with her two, three kids. The father or the mother has a car. Just Turks! Turks everywhere! So, they came, you know… they got embarrassed of how they are. And I look at my *cousin*, my aunt's daughter, she looks no different from a *bum*, who sits on the street. In terms of clothes, I mean. I don't know…um…how should I say…there is no real belief, religion, or any culture. Also no *tradition*…nothing! She's lost everything, that girl.
And…um…God forgive…then she says to me "prove that there is a god." I mean, come on, she's a Turkish girl from Turkey!

It is his (as he labels her) "gothic" cousin from Turkey, who is out of place in what he calls "Klein Istanbul," which, as he repeatedly stresses, represents an original Turkish cultural locale: "Just Turks! Turks everywhere!" Berk sharply contrasts the 'freakish' style of his cousin with a peaceful, family-friendly atmosphere. In symbolic terms, the cousin's 'scary' makeup is put in opposition to the headscarf of a mother carrying her child. By means of this opposition,

Berk points to the irony that the girl who comes from the place of cultural 'origins' has lost all connection to "belief, religion [...] culture." If, in his previous account, it was German culture where Turkish girls have lost their moral ideals, now, 'Turks' in Germany are depicted as having preserved Turkish norms and values even better than 'Turks' in Turkey have. Within this conundrum of confused contradictions, Berk implicitly raises the question of where on earth original Turkishness can be located.

It seems hardly coincidental that Berk uses the example of his cousin from Izmir. Ambiguously dislocated within Turkish cultural geography, Izmir is known because of its supposedly 'liberal,' 'modern' and 'Westernized' image and its assumed disconnection from the 'original' Anatolian tradition, because of which it is given the label 'infidel Izmir' (Saraçoğlu 2010: 73; Mansel 2010: 32). In fact, when Group A discusses the difference between 'Turks' in Turkey and 'Turks' in Germany, Funda also points to Izmir. For the participants, Izmir forms then a comparative point, a discursive variable that, on the one hand, serves to defend the norms and values practiced among 'Turks' living in Germany, and, on the other, to criticize their conservatism. In Funda's words, 'Turks' living in Germany are unaware of the "girls in Turkey, especially [of] those from Izmir. They are totally different".

By referring to Izmir, the participants differentiated 'Turks in Germany' from 'Turks in Turkey' in the sense of what Kathrin Prümm et al. describe as a narrative of "asymmetric changes" (Prümm/Sackmann/Shultz 2003: 167). Presenting their field research about "second-generation Turks in Germany," Prümm et al. point to the striking fact that among their research participants "only a few migrants include Turks who live in Turkey when they refer to 'Turks' as a group" (2003: 168). In this respect, the reference to Izmir is inherently ambivalent. While presenting a rhetoric of internal cultural difference in Turkey, it also draws on a narrative of a cultural split. As one of Prümm et al.'s interviewees remarks, 'Turks in Turkey' and 'Turks in Germany' "have become two peoples" (2003: 168).

This imaginary cultural split is also debated in Group C.

Extract 7

(Demet): I think the young people in Turkey are freer. For instance, the ones I know are going out freely. They have boyfriends. Nobody interferes. Everybody going to the university can go to other cities easily, without any problem. But here, if you want to go to other cities for the university, parents immediately ask "Why? Why are you going? Stay here!"
(?): Yes
(Demet): I think the mentality of Turkish parents remained the same. And they want to raise their kinds in the same mentality. Turks in Turkey are better in keeping pace with the West.
(Leyla): Well, in order not to loose our values, we are aware of who we are. Those who are in Turkey are not afraid of losing anything. They are more concerned with assimilating, to the West usually, in an everyone-goes-that-way-let's-go-that-way-too mentality. Here, it is just about "let's not lose [anything], we are here in a foreign country"...different, its mentality is different. We are trying not to lose it within in a different culture.

Examining the attitude of Turkish parents in Germany, Demet claims that, in comparison to parents in Turkey, 'Turkish' parents in Germany intervene too much in their children's lives. In contrast to this 'conservatism'—in her words, their "mentality remained same"—the youth in Turkey is brought up in a relatively liberal atmosphere, indicated by the possibility of easily changing one's location and having a "boyfriend." In short, Demet sees 'Turks in Turkey' as more "Western" than 'Turks in Germany'. This can be seen as a rhetorical strategy to point out the ironic dimension of narratives of cultural originality. Rather than revealing a fundamental difference between

'Turks in Turkey' and 'Turks in Germany', it primarily puts pressure on the discourse that frames Turkishness as non-Western in Germany. And it does this by positioning the supposed origin of Turkishness, that is, Turkey, as already Western.

What Demet praises, Leyla condemns. For her, 'Turks in Turkey' unreflectively assimilate to Western narratives of progress and so-called 'liberal' principles. Rather than consciously choosing their own path of cultural development, Leyla describes 'Turks in Turkey' as thoughtlessly emulating 'the West' as though following a kind of 'herd instinct'. Because, as she sees it, 'Turks in Turkey' appear as a homogenous group: "they are not afraid of losing their own culture." According to Leyla, it is exactly this cultural panic, an anti-assimilationist stance, through which 'Turks in Germany' become aware of their cultural 'origins'. Creating a we/they dichotomy, Leyla assumes that 'Turks in Germany' are able to maintain an intra-cultural cohesion because of the condition of living side-by-side with a cultural other, in the sense of what Seyla Benhabib describes as a construction of cultural "homogeneity out of narrative dissonance" (Benhabib 2002: 8).

In fact, this constitutive difference is also foregrounded in a comment by Eda, a Group B member.

Extract 8

(Eda): The place where we live in Turkey is called Etiler. We live very close to the Bosporous. When we go out with our *pardesü* (overcoat) they look at me as if I am an alien. There are no morals, no religion in Turkey! [with an angry voice]

Eda describes her experience of being excluded as a woman wearing a *pardesü*[6] in the Etiler, a neighborhood known for its predominantly 'secular-Kemalist' residents (Adaman/Ardıç 2008: 31; Pusch 2001: 203). On the other hand, her emphasis that her place is "very close to the Bosporus" is meaningful because it denotes an 'upper class' environment. This displays her translocally changing class status: while coming from a working-class family in Germany, in Turkey, she positions herself as living among the elite. In fact, for Eda, Etiler becomes a contradictory location where she experiences what Floya Anthias calls the "intersection between privilege and disadvantage": Eda is privileged in terms of class (compared to her status in Germany); yet, she is disadvantaged because, as she puts it, her *pardesü* provokes a gaze in the public space that makes her feel like an "alien" (Anthias 2012: 134).

It is interesting that, in her description of the discomfort she feels in Etiler, she does not use the term 'headscarf', since this would refer to a different discourse of exclusion in Germany.[7] This means, her choice of words calls for a distinction between what her religious dress signifies in Germany and in Turkey.[8] In both places, her veiling produces a form of what Nilüfer Göle calls "disruptive visibility," which is constituted by a paradox between the supposed function of the veil and its effect (The Disruptive Visibility of Islam in European

---

6   *Pardesü* is a specific Turkish Islamic garment, which covers the body from neck to ankle.
7   For an extensive analysis of the 'headscarf' as a discursive marker of exclusion of Muslim women in Germany, see: Weber; Beverly (2013): *Violence and Gender in the 'New' Europe: Islam in German Culture*. Basingstoke: Palgrave Macmillan.
8   This distinction becomes explicit at the end of her statement, when she implies that Etiler is a synecdochal location that reflects the absence of "morals" and "religion" in Turkey as a whole.

Publics 2011).[9] Though veiling can be understood as a performative enactment of avoiding the gaze, in the 'secular' public space, veiled women are overexposed; rather than being invisible, they attract the gaze.[10] Yet, by referring to her pardesü, Eda specifies the locationally situated constellations of this disruptive visibility. Whereas in Germany, her dress marks her as a 'Turkish woman', in Etiler, it marks her as a 'non-secular, religiously orthodox woman'. In other words, in Etiler, she feels excluded because of the very sign that positions her as 'Turkish' in Germany. In fact, this sense of belonging to neither of the two nation-states is articulated more clearly by Berk.

Extract 9

(Berk): You see, it is modernity what made them [Turks in Turkey] change like this. We don't have any homeland, we're caught in-between, when I go there [Turkey] I feel out of place. When I enter Kassel, I feel home, really.
(?): Yes, yes.
(Berk): My homeland is Kassel, in other words.

---

9 In Göle's account, Islamic veiling can be understood as a form of displaying "piety," "modesty" and "self-discipline," particularly with respect to "sexuality" (*The Disruptive Visibility of Islam in European Publics* 2011).

10 When I brought up this example in a seminar I taught at Marmara University, Istanbul, some students brilliantly pointed out that Eda might have been gazed at not only because of the fact that she is veiled, but because of her style of veiling. For Etiler is known as a neighborhood in which showing off that one lives at the pulse of fashion matters. Rather than the veil itself, its 'old fashioned' appearance might have been perceived as out of place.

Berk distances himself from both nation-states because of their forms of "modernity."[11] Instead, he expresses a sense of belonging to his immediate environment, that is, to Kassel. This can be compared to "the politics of place making," in which, according to Michael Peter Smith, "fervent urban loyalties [...] sometimes trump loyalties to nation-states" (Smith 2011: 196). In fact, in their study, Prümm et al. point to a "correlation between seeing oneself as 'German Turk' and [the] feeling that one belongs to the city" rather than to Turkey or Germany (Prümm/Sackmann/Shultz 2003: 165).

As my reading of the discussion extracts in this section suggests, in their conceptualization of LBR's performance, the participants' vision of cultural originality destabled oppositions between what counts as 'Turkish' and what not. Their articulations allude to what Floya Anthias calls "translocational positionality," which is a "contradictory and at times dialogical" form of (self)identification that "takes place in the context of [...] lived practices" within "the shifting locales of people's lives in terms of movements and flows" (Anthias 2008: 15–17). In their movements from Sivas to Duisburg, from Duisburg to Nordstadt, from Nordstadt to Taksim, from Klein-Istanbul to 'real' Istanbul, the participants rerouted and rerooted Turkishness, which itself became a migratory, translocally positioned concept, dislocated by its own ambiguous relation to modernity. But what aspect of modernity do they see in LBR's performance that made them distance themselves from it? Or in other words, what made Berk say, at the one point of the discussion, "if this is modernity, I prefer being called close-minded"?

---

11 I will eleborate on this point in the following section, in which I discuss the participants' contexualization of Europeanness and Germanness with respect to what they called "modernity."

GERMANNESS—THE SECOND PERSON 'I'

In this section, I trace the participants' conceptualization of 'Germanness' with respect to notions of modernity. Although they at times confidently referred to LBR as a German rapper, they also complicated the markers of 'Germanness'. In one of the discussion groups, the Turkish term özenti, which I conceptualize in this section as a performative enactment of Western ideals, emerged as central to the participants' positioning of LBR as being in between. Taking 'being born and raised' in a particular location as a crucial factor for one's cultural position, the participants put their own belonging into question.

Sexual Emancipation and Its Cultural Limits —Özenti Olmak

In all three group discussions, the participants perceived LBR's performance as a direct critique of the moral boundaries of 'Turks' living in Germany.

Extract 10

(Funda): *She did this...I think, she did this as a provocation.*

(Yaprak): *Yes, I think so too.*

/murmurs/

(Nisa): *But she is a lecturer!*

(Funda): *...as a provocation, against the majority, those who assimilate. Well, it is not 'assimilate', but those who do **not** assimilate.*

(Yıldız): *Hmm.*

(Funda): *The conservatives. Then she [LBR] said "I don't give a shit about you conservatives" because I think, I have never seen, such a thing, something like that...thatthere* [das da]. *And...um...I believe, she wanted to take attention. She wants to show that we, the Turks, are not only like this but we Turks are also like that. "And I don't care, whether I ashame...um...or disgrace you or not". And that's bullshit. That's mean* [asozial]*! She can do whatever she wants but...*

(Jale): *This cannot be taken seriously, I think.*

(Funda): *Yes, but I mean, in comparison to...um...what...*

(M): Can we talk Turkish again?

(Funda): *Sorry, one more sentence. /Laughs/ In comparison to this...what she did in Germany...um..which created such a fuss. Because here they are relatively more conservative.*

(Yıldız): *Oh!*

(Funda): *Had she done this in Turkey, they wouldn't even give a shit about it!*

With "general population" Funda means the majority of 'Turks' in Germany. Yet, it is not clearly discernable whether she articulates her own point of view or whether she vocalizes LBR's perspective when she describes this majority as "the conservatives." For Funda, it is LBR's grotesqueness, or, her appearance as an uncanny "das da" that, through its defamiliarizing, oppositional aesthetics, marks the majority of Turks as 'conservative'. Her positioning destabilizes the 'us/them' division that upholds the very notions of 'majority' and 'minority': "We, that is, the Turks, are not only like this, but also like that." From Funda's point of view, LBR disrupts the narrative that there is such a thing like a homogenously structured Turkish culture. In this respect, Funda's portrait of LBR brings to mind the Derridian "dangerous supplement," which, due to its excess of meaning, bears the power to transform the very relation between center and margin.[12] Creating a different center of "attention" [Aufmerksamkeit], LBR points to the processes of marginalization 'German culture' on the one hand, and a within 'Turkish culture' on the other.[13]

What Funda finds unacceptable is the extent of LBR's 'offensiveness', that is, her 'irresponsible' attack on values and norms hold dear by the majority of Turks in Germany. The distinctive words "ashaming" and "disgracing" evoke a defensive discourse of cultural cohesion. As I discussed in the previous section, this discourse of cultural cohesion is build upon the familial politics of emotion that determine a zone of negotiation and its thresholds of moral transgression. In Funda's view, LBR's performance displays a radicalism that abandons the language of negotiation necessary for the creation of coherent narratives of Turkishness. While Funda dissociates herself from "the conservatives"; she nevertheless appropriates the language of Turkish cultural moral codes. Ambiguously cusped between contrasting views on morality, she thus assumes a position of strategic orthodoxy, because, for her, a certain degree of 'conservatism' be-

---

12 In Derrida's words, "the dangerous supplement" always occurs "at the moment when it is a question of making visible a distancing which is neither the same nor an other" (Derrida 1998: 151). In my article "'Diese Bitch is' eine Gefahr': Lady Bitch Ray and the Dangerous Supplement— A Transcultural Feminist Reading," I argue that LBR's aesthetic is dangerously supplementary to the gendered framework of 'Turkishness' in Germany (Tuzcu 2013: 211).

13 Although I asked her to switch from German to Turkish, Funda continued in German, briefly ignoring my request, which signaled a rupture in the power relation between the researcher and the researched. For a detailed account of the precarious power dynamics in the empirical space, see: Pinar Tuzcu and Sina Motzek, "Kulturelle Übersetzung – Perspektiverweiterung und Irritation in mehrsprachiger Migrationsforschung," (2013).

comes a rhetorical necessity. The similar discussion occurred in Group C:

Extract 11

(Nurcan):Yes, if she is a Turk, she perhaps takes a stand against our values, our culture and religion. There is another girl, Sibel Kekilli.[14]
(?): Yes, she does something similar to this, doesn't she?
(Nurcan): Yes, she is also kind of denigrating Turkish families in her films. She shows them as if they are narrow minded. Perhaps she walks over our values and tries to prove that **she** is doing the right thing. I don't know...It is possible, if she is a Turk. I think it is.
(Havva): Or, if she has always been under pressure, she now expresses herself like this.
(Nurcan): Yes, perhaps. Possibly.
(M): What kind of pressure? Could you explain that a little further?
(Havva): May be she is an *özenti* [wanna-be]. Well, was she born and r raised here? [to Serap]
(Serap): Yes.
(Havva): See? If she was born and raised here, and if she had only German friends, maybe she desired to be like them [özendiyse].

---

14 Sibel Kekilli is a German Turkish actress who gained public recognition after her acclaimed performance in Fatih Akin's movie *Gegen die Wand* [*Head-On*]. However, as German mainstream media revealed her previous porn roles, she became a controversial figure. In fact, her statement that "violence is part of [the] life" of Turks in Germany only fueled the debate about her. The participants refer to her part in *Gegen die Wand* as 'problematic' since she portrays a suicidal, suppressed 'Turkish' girl who runs away from her patriarchal father and violent brothers.

In this extract, the discussants frame LBR's performance again as a denunciation of Turkish parents in Germany. Yet, what is distinctive here is Havva's use of the term özenti, which is untranslatable, because it encapsulates the ambiguity of being a non-Western-Westerner in a Western society. According to the Great Turkish Dictionary, özenti is described as "the effort of becoming the admired status or the effort of imitation the admired thing" (Büyük Türkçe Sözlük, online). Thus, the closest English translation of "özenti" would be "wannabe" which means, according to the Oxford Dictionary, "a person who tries to be like someone else or to fit in with a particular group of people (Oxford Dictionaries, online). That is, it is not the imitation itself, but an endeavor to imitate. However, what would be lost in such dictionary-based translation is the cultural significance of the word özenti, which is, its critical dimension with respect to the Turkish project of modernization. In this sense, özenti refers to the perceived imposition of "a political will to 'Westernize' cultural codes, lifestyles, and gender identities" (Göle 1996: 11). Therefore, the word özenti Havva uses, should be read in the context of 'Batıya Özenmek'—that is emulating the West—discourse.[15][16]

In his Cinema in Turkey, Savaş Arslan argues that özenti denotes the process of cultural (self)colonization that marks Turkey's ambiguous "relation to the West" (Arslan 2010: 130). Rather than being a critique of modernization as such, the term is used for those, within Turkish culture, who seem to unquestioningly submit to and fetishize the Western ideals of progress and emancipation. As Arslan writes, özenti describes the "desire to be like the other, the West" (Arslan 2010: 19). Etymologically, özenti derives from "öz" which means es-

---

15 For a detailed elaboration on the historical background of the discourse of 'Emulating the West', see: Nilüfer Göle, *The Forbidden Modern: Veiling and Civilization* (1996).

16 Havva's use of the word *özenti* evokes Leyla's phrase "everyone-goes-that-way-let's-go-that-way-too mentality" which I analyzed earlier in this chapter, see: Excerpt 7, p. 17.

sence, origin or unchangeable substance. Thus, özenti reflects the will of changing one's öz. Yet, because this remains impossible, özenti is the state in which one maintains a "double existence, not being one nor being the other but in continual movement between the two" (Arslan 2010: 19). In this respect, the verb özenmek is not just 'to imitate' or 'to emulate'.[17] Rather, it can be understood as a form of doing essence, that is, a performative act in which one puts one's 'original' identity under erasure—of constructing an öz. In this form öz signifies "desiring and relating to an alterity which is in this case the question of Being—or Being under erasure" (Spivak 1998: l).[18] In this respect, özenti is the "partial or double 'self'" that Homi K. Bhabha describes as being constitutive of mimicry. Like mimicry, özenti depends on a positional play, a deferral of identification wherein the self remains only partially recognizable. It is this partial recognizability that made Leyla say that "she [LBR] doesn't look like a Turk":

Extract 12

(Havva): I've heard that other one before, what was her name again?
(Leyla/Demet): Sibel Kekilli [simultaneously]
(?): she also won a prize.
(Havva): But, I haven't heard about this one. Yes.
(M): What could be the reason for this, in your opinion? She even comes from a Turkish family. And, as Serap also said,

---

17 Arslan also gives the etymological analysis of 'özenmek'. He writes, in Turkish, the '–enmek' suffix indicates a continuation (Arslan 2010: 128).
18 In her preface to *Of Grammatology*, Spivak explains Derrida's conceptualization of "under erasure" [*sous rature*] as a sign that is "inaccurate yet necessary" (1998: xiv). Accordingly, the act of putting meaning under erasure is "to write a word, cross it out, and then print both word and deletion. (Since the word is inaccurate, it is crossed out. Since it is necessary, it remains legible)" (1998: xiv).

> she is doing something like breaking taboos, in terms of sexuality so on so. Why is this?
>
> (Leyla): Honestly, it is not noticeable that she is a Turk. We could say yes this girl is Turk, if **at least** her name was Turkish or if there were something that symbolizes Turkey. But when you said it then...Well, she doesn't look like a Turk. Perhaps, that's why. Her name is different. And it is also not noticeable from her style of talk.

Answering my question, Leyla claims that it is LBR's name, her way of talking (Leyla refers to LBR's accent-free German) and the absence of Turkish symbols in her performance that render her Turkishness indiscernible. This means, what obscures LBR's Turkishness, for Leyla, is her style, her gestures. It is not her physical appearance, but her acting that determines her cultural (not)belonging. The similar topic came up in Group A:

Extract 13

> (Nisa): You would have never known that she is Turkish.
>
> (Funda): Yes, without knowing this, it doesn't make any sense, perhaps. But after learning that [she is a Turk], it arouses your interest.

Funda stresses the importance of knowing LBR's cultural background in order to make sense of her performance, because, as she implies, it is inseparable from and performatively entangled with her sexual explicitness. This fundamental complementarity in her performance highlights the process by which supposedly original Turkishness both comes into being and is under erasure. While LBR's references to a form of Turkishness endow her porn-aesthetic with directly politicized meaning, her sexual explicitness provokes a re-assessment of the meaning of Turkishness.

Extract 14

(Yıldız): That *ambience* wasn't European style. That was rather something else. I mean, it it were European, it would be more like...well...*it was rather in the direction of*...Eastern cultural stuff...how can I say...rather like Eastern cultural, like Turkey, but rather like Eastern Turkey [Jale and Ceren exchange glances][19]. Such a culture. Well, somehow it goes in that direction...
(Jale): Hmm, well but...
(Yıldız): Well, it doesn't have to be Turkey. But, it was not kinda European cultural, I think.
/Murmuring/
(Nisa): I missed that totally.
(Yaprak): So did I.
(Jale): Hmm.
(Yıldız): When I saw it the first time, this was what I recognized. How to say...in other clips for instance...well, for instance, well, it is also different from the clips made by Germans. I mean when it isn't modern, it should be oriental. But it wasn't **oriental** either. *It was some sort of mixture of something* [War irgendwo so eine Gemisch von was]...I don't know...That's what I noticed...

Yildiz's description of the music video draws attention to its ambiguous aesthetics. What she refers to as its ambience, the aesthetic tone, gives, for her, a sense of indeterminateness. It is as if it incorporates aesthetically LBR's positional play. It is neither this nor that, but

---

19 The participants' exchange of glances is significant since it speaks for the diversity inside the group that is silently articulated. Ceren and Jale' gesture make Yildiz to revisit her statement to take back its might-be-offensive effect on her coparticipants. I discuss this issue in chapter 2 in line with the importance of transcultural translation of gestures as silent articulations.

"some sort of mixture" that cannot be clearly named, only sensed, "noticed."

Almost the Same but Not Quite

While emphasizing that LBR transgresses the gendered norms of Turkishness, the participants also question whether she could be categorized as German. As Yildiz says, Germans, too, "call such things sittenwidrig (indecent)". At another point of the discussion, Yildiz uses the word sittenwidrig again as to underline the degree of transgressive act of LBR's performance.[20]

Extract 15

(Ceren): Yes, *this doesn't fit into societal norms.*
(Nisa): *Yes indeed. This doesn't fit into* neither of them.
(Ceren): *This simply doesn't fit into society.*
(Yıldız): I think this has nothing to do with religion. It's something about **culture**, like *sittenwidrig, immoral.*
(Ceren): *judgmental...*
(Nisa): Can be both at the same time.

---

20 In the German context, the word *Sittenwidrigkeit* is used as a juridical term. The *German Civil Code [Bürgerliches Gesetzbuch]* defines *Sittenwidrigkeit* as a "violation of good morals [Verstoß gegen die guten Sitten]" (para. 138). Yildiz's use of the term is by means coincidental here. As Sarah Kovner shows in her study, *Sittenwidrigkeit* is fraught with sexual connotations. For instance, until recently, the term *Sittenwidrigkeit* was used with a reference to prostitution in *German Civil Code* (Kovner 2012: 145). For a thorough analysis of the rhetoric of *Sittenwidrigkeit* in German context, see: Bernhard Pichler's *Sex als Arbeit: Prostitution als Tätigkeit im Sinne des Arbeitsrechts* (2013), and Margaret Sönser Breen and Fiona Peters' *Genealogies of Identity: Interdisciplinary Readings on Sex and Sexuality* (2005).

(Yıldız): *Exactly!*
(Funda): *Values and norms.*
Rather than just transgressing the strictures of what counts as being Turkish, LBR's performance is seen as not fitting in generally. After Ceren points out that LBR's sexual politics cannot be simplistically extrapolated from and reduced to her cultural background, the participants agree that LBR reaches beyond the cultural territory of Turkishness and therefore targets "values and norms" of German society as a whole. What is remarkable here is that the participants use the German expression sittenwidrig, which ambivalently coincides with their framing of LBR's performance with the Turkish expression ahlak dışı (indecent). The ambivalence in the relation between Turkish and German values is particularly pronounced in the following extract from Group C:

Extract 16

(Nurcan): Well, here Germans say integr..*integrate* yourself.. we say we want to preserve our values..You see some Turks who are not exactly Turkish not exactly German, they are in-between. I don't know..well, do you mean [to Serap] this girl doesn't know where she belongs to? I think she knows it very well! She apparently embraced German culture [laughs]
(?): But, there is also no such thing in Germany either.
(Nurcan): Or… European culture.. let's say she assimilated to European culture
(silence)
(Havva): Not every German is like that if you think..
(Nurcan): Yes, you're right, they aren't. For sure, they also have…I actually didn't mean it that way. They also have a certain degree of morality and decency
(Havva): They also have certain cultural norms.
(Nurcan): Sure! They also have a sense of shame.

(?): Yes!
(?): Right!
(Nurcan): They do have some limits. Yes.
(silence)
(Havva): But I still wonder how her parents reacted. I'm really curious
(Laughs)
(Serap): I guess she doesn't have contact to them anymore. Imagine that she's doing such things for many years as far as I know.
(Leyla): See? We don't support such things. Well, sure Germans would also give a certain reaction to this. Even though they are German, nobody would like to see their daughter like this. But..still..they wouldn't exclude her that much. "Well, my daughter is doing such things, because she has different ideas"...but we...well, see? It immediately took our attention. We ask "what did her parents do?" we wonder such things. Because such things are rejected in our culture. It's not accepted.
(Nurcan): *Ahlak dışı*, one might say.

For a moment, for Nurcan, LBR's cultural belonging seems to be clear. It is her sexual explicitness that unambiguously displays her identification with German culture. Yet, this neat categorization is immediately challenged and, being confronted with strong reactions, Nurcan revokes the essentializing tone in her language by saying Germans "also have a certain degree of morality and decency." This is echoed by her coparticipants, who assert that German culture has "certain cultural norms," "some limits," and "a sense of shame," too. Evoking the theme of Sittenwidrigkeit in Group A, these phrases complicate the distinction between Turkish and German culture. That is to say, discarding the opposition between total restriction and moral mayhem, the participants underline shared boundaries, with respect to the visibility of sexuality in the public sphere. In fact, through this, their own position loses a sense of marginality, as they include themselves within a broader cultural framework based on the limits that LBR's aesthetic seems to defy and surpass.

Then, what is, according to the participants, the impulse for this defiance? Is it, as Nurcan asks Serap, because "she doesn't know where she belongs to"?

Extract 17

(Serap): I think this woman is *simply* doing what she wants to do. Well, think about our Turkish culture. In our culture, it's like, women don't desire sexual intercourse so much. They don't want it that much. That's why there are so many *divorces*. That's why...she was born and raised in Europe and that's why prefers to be more liberated. Because it is usual in our culture to say "oh, don't do this, this is forbidden, that's forbidden"...hm...how to say?
(M): say it in German
(Serap): she *simply* didn't *embrace* this [Turkish] culture. [o kültürü *einfach annehmen* yapmadı]

In Serap's words, it is not just about knowing or not knowing where one belongs to. Rather, LBR chose not to "embrace" Turkish culture because of its gender-biased requirements, particularly regarding sexuality. While Nurcan, as I earlier discussed, sees these gendered requirements as a result of parental misinterpretation of cultural codes, Serap describes gender-biased restriction as "usual" in Turkish culture.[21] Yet, Serap does not affirm an absolute voluntarism, for she concedes that a culturally diverse milieu can lead to a certain degree of confusion.

---

21 For Nurcan's complete statement, see: Extract 2.

Extract 18

(Serap): But, I can say this. In Germany there is not only one German culture. There are also Italy, *Italians,* Italy *well,* people who are from *Italy*...and there are also Russians. In Germany, there are really many different cultures. People those who are born here but whose mothers are from Italy, they don't know what culture they should adapt to. Should they adapt to the culture here or should they adapt to their mothers' culture? They also don't want to let their mothers down. But some norms of that culture [mother's culture] go unheed...unheede...unheeded here [pronunciation difficulty] /laughs/. That's why we...they... have some difficulties. That's why this girl in this music video [LBR] makes these kind of videos and writes these kinds of texts.
(M): Why? Do you mean she does this to highlight these difficulties?
(Serap): She doesn't have a stable personality. She doesn't know what she wants. She's born and raised in Europe, on the one hand, and she encounters different cultures, on the other. Well, all of them [cultures] seem very attractive to her. But you can't adapt to all of them at the same time, because they're all different. In the end, you have to choose one. There's only one way, not three.

Besides repeating the point that LBR representation is symptomatic of a state of confusion, Serap refers to Germany as a transcultural space, not just constituted by an oppositional relation between Turkishness and Germanness, but, rather, a space that is impacted on by various cultural differences—"there are also...Italians...and there are also Russians." Significant is also that she maternalizes cultural difference. Once again, one's positionality in relation to cultural difference is implicated in an affective dynamic within the family. However, whereas Selin rhetorically anchored this affective dynamic in the figure of the father—being able to "look [one's] father in the eyes"—Serap does this in the figure of the mother.[22] Her point is that one is positioned in a pre-established spectrum of choices in which one culture is valued over another. Through that, certain cultural practices are relegated to invisibility—they "go unheeded." And one is always placed on a crossroads, assumed to choose and determine one's belonging, because "in the end," as she puts it, cultural markers are supposed to be one-directional: "there's only one way, not three." Ironically, the quick shift of the subject in Serap's phrase—from we to they—sheds a flash of light on the participants' own, hitherto only vaguely present, form of positioning. In other words, if cultural inbetweenness has heretofore been kept at a certain distance, signaled by self-detaching, otherizing phrases like "some," "those who," "they" and "them," Serap's rhetorical slip illuminates an ambivalent relation between the narrator and the narrated. In an exchange between Berk and Zeynep (Group B), this ambivalence becomes more explicit in an affective shift that disrupts their mode of not-me-positioning.

Extract 19

(Berk): Well, that girl [LBR], has she been living in Turkey or in Germany?
(Zeynep): She was born and raised here.
(Berk): Obviously.
(Zeynep): I was also born and raised here. What's so obvious? What are you trying to say?

Zeynep's cornering of Berk makes one pause. For are they not all born and raised in Germany as well? Are the gendered markers that "obvious" that one can make a clear-cut distinction between assimilation and cultural allegiance? What I am trying to say is that the essen-

---

22 For Selin's complete statement, see: Extract 1.

tializing rhetoric about belonging and cultural ascription turns out to be tenuous and too fragile to uphold a distinction between Germanness and Turkishness. In other words, the shift in tone occurring in Zeynep and Berk's confrontation relocates the question of what determines one's Germanness. From a question between self and Other, it turns into an immediate positional relation between an I and a You ["I was also born and raised here," says Zeynep, "What are you trying to say"]. This relation surfaces as a positionality impossible to project onto a distanced Other—in this case LBR. Therefore, distancing oneself from Germanness collapses into a form of distancing from one another and, indeed, from themselves. In this situated moment, then, German identity becomes a second person I. I am borrowing here the Japanese-German poet Yoko Tawada's phrase "Die zweite Person Ich," which describes the creation of an ambiguous attachment. That is to say, secondary here does not mean minor and of lower rank. Instead it stands for the deconstruction of the mode of identification inscribed in grammar. That is to say, rather than splitting the I as first and second, it seeks for a new language to reposition the I and the You as complimentary. In this dialogue, the participants' momentary construction of Germannes emerges from this complementary form of positioning. Zeynep's "I was also born in raised here" does not only refer to Lady Bitch Ray, but also to Berk. In this moment, identity construction through self-other dynamics collapses and transforms into an ambiguous I and You, I as You, and You as I.

Although the participants use distinctive categories of Germanness and Turkishness, they also challenge and reassess the very conditions of what reinforces and rigidifies these categories. By labeling LBR as özenti, the participants emphasize an inescapability of the cultural identity one is supposed to enact simply because one is "born into and raised within" a certain cultural context. However, in their reading, being özenti becomes a performative act that signifies a desire to move away from one's origins, and through this, subverts and obscures the recognizability of these origins. This means, being özenti is a simulation of a cultural belonging by means of an enactment of not-belonging. Produced by LBR's sexual explicitness, this ambiguity unfolds not merely as a transgression of gendered norms of Turkishness but, as the participants stress, also as a defiance of the form of visibility of sexuality in German culture as a whole. In fact, the very attempt to make sense of this broader defiance of gendered norms reoriented the discussions towards feminist topoi.

FEMINISM—APOSIOPETIC POSITIONING

After rewatching the clip, each group moved the overall angle of the discussion away from questions of cultural belonging towards questions of gender inequality, emancipation of women, sexual freedom and the representation of women in popular culture. The participants those who, ambiguously, seemed to assume an unswervingly oppositional stance towards LBR's aesthetic reconsidered their posture when it came to the issue of feminist politics. This can be noticed, for instance, in the change of Yildiz's position.

Extract 20

(Yıldız): I think, on the other hand, the clip has **one good cause.** When you look at those RnB and HipHop artists, generally, women are represented as weak and as *victims*. This, however, is more like "you can do only as much as I can do with you," something like that.

(?): Yes

(Yıldız): Or, *along the lines of "I'll give it to you..."*

(Funda): Yes, yes.

(Yıldız): What happens here is exactly the opposite. It's about her, about women.

(Funda): "You're not a real man."

(Yıldız): Well, because they always typecast women as weak, it seems as if she wants to show and say: "No, women can achieve something as well, regardless what it is and who she is."

(Yaprak): Well, but then again, she just shows how this kind of video could only have been shot by a man. So there's no difference. Either way she's just a slut, regardless if a rapper sings or she herself sings. Either way, she just shows herself.

(Yıldız): *But she wants to teach the ins and outs...and she doesn't want to show that it are the men who are teaching the ins and outs* [*zeigen wo es langgeht*]. This is what I mean.

(Yaprak): Yes, that's true! but nevertheless, she's still showing herself.

(Yıldız): Well, *the power is in her hands*. That's what she wants to show.

At the very beginning of Group A's discussion, Yildiz started the debate with a categorical rejection. Leaning back with crossed arms, she said assuredly, "This is a disgrace!" After watching the clip a second time, she showed a sense of realignment, moving from merely judging LBR's performance with words like "utanç" and "sittenwidrig," towards a position of understanding, commenting on the clip's "good cause."[23] Referring to HipHop and RnB music videos, she goes into women's representation in popular culture, explaining to her coparticipants what she sees as a form of feminist agency in LBR's performance. According to her, the video gives a sense of a

---

23 However, this does by no means indicate that Yildiz abandons her previous position for good. Rather, as her following statements show, she holds multiple positions at once.

power reversal, displaying a woman who teaches men "the ins and outs." A similar positional shift occured in Group B.

Extract 21

(Berk): As Zeynep said, she means...it's like, *socially* women are oppressed, for instance, I earn three times more than you earn, always men occupy the highest positions and so on. This is what feminism is about. Being against such things.
(Selin): Yes, yes, ok! I got it! But do we agree with it or not, this is what I didn't understand.
(Zeynep): Aha! Well, Lady Bitch Ray does this against those.
(Selin): hmmm
(?): Now she got it!
(Berk): Well, there was some kind of injustice she encountered. Now she takes her revenge
(Selin): I don't agree!
(Mehtap): Neither do I. A person who encountered injustice would accomplish that much...
(Zeynep): We don't say that she herself encountered injustice. Maybe she witnessed it in her environment. Now, she's *coming to terms with* [*verarbeiten*] it.
(Berk): Exactly, exactly. For instance, she witnessed these things in her everyday life. Well, it's true that there are always men who occupy the highest positions in work places. Okay...there's also Merkel, for example, who governs entire Europe. And perhaps, this idiot [LBR] hasn't noticed this yet.
(Mehtap): But that happens rarely.
(Zeynep): This is just a *theory* of mine. I don't claim that it is true for sure.
(Berk): Okay, yes! I agree with you too [to Zeynep] I support you in this issue! I'm actually trying to back you up on this [sabahtan beri]

Giving his definition of feminism, Berk describes what he perceives as LBR's central motive. According to him, LBR's performance revolts—takes "revenge"—against broader societal gender inequalities. While previously holding the most apparently polarized opinions in Group B's discussion, Berk and Zeynep now side with one another and, as Zeynep's "we" indicates, they jointly argue for recognizing LBR's feminist cause.

This debate over the feminist politics in LBR's performance can be compared to statements made early on in Group A's discussion.

Extract 22

(Nisa): I didn't know her either. I've just heard about Sibel Kekilli.
(Yıldız): Yes, only about her.
/Laughing/
(Nisa): I didn't hear about anyone else.
(Jale): But what she [Sibel Kekilli] did, was something rather different.
(Yıldız): Yes.
(Nisa): But anybody else.
(Yaprak): *Yes, she did porn-movies.*
(Yıldız): Yes. This is exactly...this is what I wanted to say. This, what she's doing can be classified as *pornography*. But about her [LBR] you don't even know what to say, whether this is a kind of liberal art [açık sanat] or something on its own....something like...
(Jale): She is a rap-artist.
(Yıldız): *I can't categorize her.*

Referring to porn, the participants attempt to categorize the aesthetic of the music video. As Jale makes clear, a certain distinction has to be drawn between Sibel Kekilli and LBR. While, for them, the former belongs unquestionably to the porn genre, the latter is, as Yildiz says, difficult to classify because of the clip's irresolvable aesthetic tension between porn-like vulgarity and a sense of artistic (political) intention. Jale's term "rap-artist" only vaguely captures this tension. However, the participants come up with a concrete example.

Extract 23

(Jale): Do you know any other artist, who is similar to her?
(Funda): You mean as a woman?
(Yaprak): As a woman, *if any, only Lil' Kim would go in that direction.*
(Funda): Yes.
(Yaprak): *But otherwise*, I don't know anyone else
(Funda): As a man...
(Yaprak): Aha! As a man? Ohoooooo [Turkish expression] tons of them. But as a woman...
(Funda): Lil´Kim!
(Yaprak): Yes!
(Nisa): I don't know any
(Ceren): Yes, of course! That's right! Lil´Kim!

As the rapper who, as Greg Thomas writes, "invented" a style that foregrounds female "sexual self-determination," Lil' Kim is brought up as the only comparative figure. The participants underline the male-dominance visible in HipHop discourse. At another point of the discussion, Funda provides examples from the German rap scene, mentioning King Orgasmus and TAK.[24] Finding their only female

---

24 King Orgasmus and TAK are two porn-rappers with explicit, misogynistic lyrics. In Germany, this music genre is also referred to under the title of '*Arschficksongs*'. In her tracks, LBR mostly counter-attacks these rappers. For further analysis of LBR's lyrics in relation to the German Hip Hop scene, see: Pinar Tuzcu, "'Diese Bitch is' eine Gefahr': Lady Bitch Ray and the Dangerous Supplement—A Transcultural Locational Feminist Reading," (2013).

example in the US, the participants point to LBR's uniqueness, particularly in a German pop-cultural context. A direct link between LBR and Lil' Kim is established in the participants' discussion of the two rappers' similar mode self-naming via a reappropriation of the word 'bitch'.[25]

Extract 24

(Berk): That's a provocation.
(Zeynep): Yes, she wants to say I'm different. I'm not like those Turkish girls that you know
(Berk): "Be a bitch" she means
(Zeynep): No, she doesn't say "be a bitch." She's denigrating men. That's why I see her as a feminist
(Eda): But she says it *implicitly*.
(Zeynep): She says it both *explicitly* and *implicitly*. She has also other music videos. I watched those too.
(Berk): But she ends up with a man anyway.
(Zeynep): So what? But on her own terms. She says "nobody can force me to do so." This means sexual freedom; she has a feminist spirit.
(Berk): Sexual freedom [ironically]
(Zeynep): Yes, that's it! [smiling]
(Berk): Does she have sex with anyone she wants? *Tövbe estagfurullah* [God forgive me]
(Zeynep): Yes, but only with whom she wants.
(Berk): Then she should do it! This means that we're right, she's a bitch!
(Selin): But she already calls herself a bitch.
(Berk): That's something else!

---

25 In Chapter 1, I discuss the reappropriation of the word 'bitch' with respect to postfeminism and Hip-Hop feminism.

(Zeynep): So there is no need for us to call her a bitch.
(Selin): She knows very well what it means what she does.

What is debated in this extract from Group B is the political force of reappropriation of the term 'bitch'. The fact that LBR calls herself "already" a bitch forestalls and voids the denigration in Berk's labeling her as a "bitch." Berk himself notices this différence when he adds in lowered voice, "that's something else." It is this productive elseness in the word 'bitch' that makes him identify LBR's performance as a "provocation." As if responding to Selin's remark that LBR "knows very well what it means what she does," Ceren, from Group A, says "she defines bitch differently".

Extract 25

(Funda): *I know.* [faint smile]
(Ceren): *She doesn't see this...hmm...not like this Schlampendasein* [sluttiness], *but rather she defines being a bitch totally differently.*
(M): *But how?*
(Ceren): *I can't remember exactly. But there was, a long time ago. There was an interview*
(Funda): *Three years ago.*
(Ceren): *Yes, that's possible. It was on RTL "Explosiv."* There she gave an interview and there *she said this. In fact, her name Lady Bitch Ray, but for her this bitchiness hasn't anything to do with a **billige** Dasein* [being cheap]. But what she said exactly, I've forgotten now.
(Funda): *That's right! I also watch this on...that thing... on Youtube...that she was there.*
(Ceren): *Yes, exactly.* There she said this.
(Funda): Yes. There she talked, but what she said [clicks her tongue] is not that important.
/chuckling /

(Funda): *But the actual definition of bitch remains bitch. You can't change it. As long as the majority uses it in that way, then she can't do anything against it as an individual.*

For Ceren her, LBR rids the word 'bitch' of its existing connotations. It is not just a question of what the reappropriated meaning of 'bitch' exactly is, but primarily a question of what it is not. That is to say, in this mode of use, the word 'bitch' subverts its negative, denigrating connotations described by Ceren as "Schlampendasein" and "billige[s] Dasein." In contrast, LBR's use of the word 'bitch' signals a performative strategy. This is also hinted at by Nurcan when she says with an approving look in my direction, "it is actually worthy to make a research about why a woman calls herself a bitch," especially a woman, who, as Nisa remarks, "is a lecturer".

LBR's academic career played an important role in the participants' assessment of her moral and political standpoint. After watching the clip for the second time, Yaprak says:

Extract 26

(Yaprak): [..] I think she's a lecturer, writing her dissertation. It's clear that she doesn't just have a stupid *marketing strategy*. For what kind of *label* she's working...that they don't do this for no reason is clear. She wants to do that, too. She's developed a clever idea, an idea she herself deems as clever...um...and she wants to go on this way, so she should go on.

Yaprak's emphasis on LBR's intellectual background defers their judgmental stance towards the sexual explicitness of the performance. Rather than just being a "stupid marketing strategy"—with a mere 'sex sells' approach—LBR's porn aesthetics acquires a sense of political motivation. As Yaprak puts it, the performance is not done "for no reason."

In each group, the participants highlighted the amateurish style of the video. Remarking on the cinematography and other technical aspects such as acting, mise-en-scène, and production in general, the participants stressed that, given its 'poor' quality, the clip must have been done for other, politically and artistically motivated reasons. This means, for them, these stylistic shortcomings, that is, the failure to meet contemporary aesthetic standards became the very medium of the clip's message. The clips 'failures' thus became part and parcel of LBR's feminist intervention: they described it as a gender-swapped parody of male-dominated HipHop culture and an attack on misogynist representation of women in mainstream media. In fact, for them, this artistic dimension of the clip—or, as Yaprak puts it, LBR's "clever idea"—also explains its, at first glance, offensive vulgarity. Similarly, Berk voices also a sudden recognition:

Extract 27

(Berk): You know what? She is much cleverer than we think she is.
(?): Yes
(Zeynep): Yes, she really is clever. She says "I'm a woman and I represent womanhood." She says, "I'm not representing the models on television," "I'm overweight," she says. This means *I'm not ashamed of my body* [Ich stehe zur meinem Körper]…she empowers girls who are in puberty.
(Berk): Empowers?! [ironically]
(Zeynep): Because she uses extreme sexuality, you can of course think that you don't want to represent her [UG]…but at many points… well, if you make some research, at many points she is really good. It's just like she is giving a punch on your face…hitting you on your top of your head. If she were a little bit calmer, what she says is quite right actually, not wrong.

Berk's statement prompts Zeynep to explain the political dimension of the performance. According to her, it displays a certain body politics, a resistance to how the female body is represented in popular culture. After Berk challenges her choice of words—"empowerment"—Zeynep explains that LBR's body politics cannot be reduced to what she describes as "extreme sexuality." Rather it is her rebellious and over-the-top confrontational attitude that manifests her feminist objective. Though easily overshadowed by her overtly sexualized aesthetics, at a fundamental level, Zeynep says, LBR's feminist message is "quite right."

If for Zeynep this feminist message is a general attempt to empower pubescent girls, Jale (Group A) points out that it has to be read in relation to its cultural specificity.

Extract 28

(Jale): It's no coincidence that she comes from Turkey and shows her emancipation like this. And she comes also from Turkey. Well, and I consider the relation to religion also not as a coincidence.

Jale maintains that LBR spectacularizes female sexual emancipation not despite, but precisely because "she comes from Turkey." Thus, LBR's performance subverts the stereotypes attached to the image of Turkishness in Germany. What LBR does, in Jale's view, is revealing the diversity within what is assumed a homogenous Turkish culture in Germany. Esin (Group B), however, sees a risk in LBR's strategy.

Extract 29

(Esin): As Zeynep says, she [LBR] assumes that Turkish girls are under pressure of their parents. That's why she makes such a music video and gives a massage "actually it is like this too." This is what modernleşmek [becoming modern] is.

(Selin): ok, but...
(Zeynep): What she wants to say is sexual freedom...sexual freedom for women
(Berk): Yes!
(Eda): I think she is a kind of educated cahil [primitive]
(Esin): What she says is...well...don't get married görücü usulü [prearranged marriage] but sleep around with guys and then get married.
(Berk): Calm down bacim [my sister], calm down...
(Zeynep): With a feminist approach...
(Selin): Well, actually I love *feminist*s! But if this is *feminism*...
(Zeynep): She is a *feminist*, too!
(Selin): Come on, what kind of a *feminist* is she? This is just about being a slut [orospuluk].
(Zeynep): But, she really is *a feminist*
(Selin): I am so sorry, I was pissed off! [to me]
(M): No, no, there is no need to apologize.
(Zeynep): But she is! *What she says*...look, her *label* is called *Vagina Kunst. What does it mean? It means she takes a stand* ...she takes a stand for her sexual emancipation.
(Eda): Yes, it's clear she is a feminist.

If, in Jale's view, LBR's spectacularization of female emancipation disrupts stereotypes of Turkishness, in Esin's view, it reinforces these stereotypes by displaying sexual explicitness as the catchall formula for liberation. This formula is, as Esin says, a fundamental part of the hegemonically imposed Western ideal of modernization. It is this normative vision of emancipation through which other modalities of agency are silenced. Therefore, according to Esin, LBR's performance reproduces the very polarization between, on the one hand, an image of Turkishness marked by restriction and prearranged marriage, and, on the other, a Western-cultural discourse of promiscuity.

However, rather than debating on whether the performance can be described as feminist, the participants asked, in Selin's words, "what kind of a feminist" LBR is. What is under critique, then, is not feminism as such, but the form of feminism LBR represents. While, for instance, Zeynep evokes a post-feminist discourse by claiming that LBR's assertion of female agency is encoded in the name of her record label ("Vagina Kunst"), Selin disapproves of the performance's objectification of the female body. When Selin says that she "loves feminists" her choice of word "actually" signifies a potential contradiction. It marks a point at which she senses the necessity to declare her love of feminism, precisely because, as a 'Turkish' girl in Germany, she is pre-positioned as inherently deficient of a feminist mindset. And the mode of her positioning is aposiopetic—open and unfinished—ambiguously marked with the silence that breaks off her sentence: "actually I love feminists! But if this is feminism…"

Pointing at the Limits of Existing Discourses

What Selin left unsaid in the context of feminism, Berk articulates without hesitation when it comes to the question of modernity: "if this is modernity," he says, "I prefer to be called close-minded". In both situations, the participants encounter a discursive gap that does preclude a 'third' choice: if one disapproves 'sexual freedom', a term charged with notions of promiscuity, one cannot be a 'feminist'. Or, similarly, if one rejects the normative ideals of modernity, one wears the tag of being 'close-minded'.

In Group A, these processes of mutual exclusion are problematized more clearly. The participants' cautious, contradictory, and critical use of certain terms such as 'normal,' 'open-minded', and 'tolerant' marked the edges of immediately available discursive domains and their positional binaries.

Extract 30

(Yaprak): She is one of those for whom it backlashed.
(M):   How does that happen, that backlash?

(Yaprak): Well, I don't know, you know…
(Funda): When you are a kid…
(Yaprak): Some, some…um…I don't know. *A bad example, or two examples.* On the one hand a mother and a father are very [acayip] religious, you see, *very* [richtig] very [acayip] religious [dindar]. *Well, I don't know how I should define that.* This family constrains the kid. Then that backfires. On the other hand, when the parents are very open-minded, the girl…girl or boy, whatever…needs to hold on to something [dala tutunmak] and therefore becomes religious [dindar]. *That also exists.* That's a backlash.

Describing LBR's performance as a "backlash" against the moral values imposed on her by her family, Yaprak does not clearly define the characteristics of what she calls "extremely religious." Recognizing the rhetorical trap of assigning certain cultural codes—such as the headscarf—to distinct moral camps within Turkish culture, Yaprak just repeats the adjective "extremely" in both languages (richtig, acayip). Moreover, by invalidating her point prior to its articulation—"a bad example"—she marks the discursive boundaries that would fix her position in a certain discourse on Turkish culture. That is why she points to an inability to "define" what exactly causes the "backlash." She even further invalidates her point by giving an oppositional example, in which a "very open-minded" upbringing can also be disadvantageous. Contrary to her hesitation in her first example, here, however, she insists on the validity of her argument: "That also exists." In this rhetorical move, Yaprak distances herself from the dichotomous narratives of either 'conservatism' or 'open-mindedness'. While Yaprak remained ambiguous, Nisa affirmed this binary more confidently.

Extract 31

(Nisa): Perhaps her family, really very, you know...I don't know, perhaps they use headscarves. Perhaps they are religious [dinci]. And that has backfired. Perhaps, they are completely...maybe her family is normal too. Well, what I mean with 'normal' is like her [LBR], you know?
(Funda): Open, open...
(Nisa): Open-minded perhaps, but you know...

Because it unguardedly opposes "normal" and "open-minded" to "religious," (symbolized by the "headscarf") Nisa's statement meets irritation and disapproval, which can especially be seen in Yildiz's response.

Extract 32

(Yıldız): You all speak about open-mindedness, tolerance. But I think this has nothing to do with open-mindedness. Not in the least.
(Nisa): No, no! You are right the correct word is not 'open-minded'. That's right!

According to Yildiz, the very language that makes use of the term 'open-mindedness' is inapplicable with respect to LBR's performance. Therefore, she cautions her coparticipants that by labeling LBR as "free-thinking," "tolerant," or "open-mined," their own position would inevitably be locked into stereotyping notions of being 'conservative' and 'narrow-minded'. Yet, inadvertently, later on in the discussion, Yildiz herself resorts to the pre-defined discourse that she warns Nisa to avoid.

Extract 33

(Funda): Does she have a boyfriend?
(Yıldız): Um, that's possible. There's definitely someone, who thinks as permissively as she does…who is really tolerant. Why not?
(Yaprak): Please let's not call that tolerant thinking, please!
(Yıldız): Yes, now I've said that again. No, then I don't mean someone who is open-minded, but rather someone who lives at an extreme point, exactly like she does.
/laughs/
(Nisa): An extreme point. I like that.
/silence/
(Jale): But even that is ultimately also a perspective, a way of thinking.
(Yıldız): Yes it is. But it has nothing to do with being tolerant or open-minded. She's right. It has nothing at all to do with tolerant thinking.
(Nisa): Yes, there she's right.

This time it is Yaprak who warns Yildiz about the discursive deadlock. Correcting herself, and attempting to fill the discursive gap they are facing, Yildiz rephrases her statement and calls the "way of thinking" in question as positioned at "an extreme point."

Interestingly, the language in the German citizenship test is perhaps one of the clearest example through which we can explain what the participants try to avoid here. In her analysis of the German citizenship test, Yasemin Yıldız, a Turkish-German scholar, argues that, in these tests, "sexual identity" serves "as a key category" in order to assess who is tolerant enough to deserve citizen status (Yıldız 2011: 82). As her analysis reveals, because the questions are formulated in a way, they imply that "the applicants are sexist, misogynist [and] homophobic" (ibid: 82). This means that minorities are, as Yasemin Yıldız puts it, "cast as deficient of tolerance" (ibid: 83). In this respect, analyzing the sexually explicit content of the video, the participants react to the performance as if they are in a circumstance of being tested. Therefore, in order not to be trapped by these pre-established positions, they try to redefine these terms, or keep silent.[26] By reformulating tolerance and open-mindedness (and, in fact, detaching the meaning of these terms from notions of sexual freedom) they also touch a Western feminist nerve, because they question the very foundation of what counts as an emancipated 'modern' woman in Western societies. Being particularly cautious in handling these terms, the participants challenge this discursive limit by refusing the prescribed way of framing one's stance towards issues of gender and sexuality. In other words, their concept—the "extreme point"—becomes an alternative to what is available.[27] This extreme point however remains an ambiguous abstraction, a "vague position" that, in Christian Metz's words, "may be precise as the outline of a 'problematic'" (Metz 1974: 139). It is exactly this vagueness of the term which signals something emerging, something that cannot yet be articulated. In this sense, the "extreme point" becomes a Not Yet that "expresses what exists as mere tendency, a movement that is latent in the very process of manifesting itself," questioning and redetermining what can and what cannot be said (Santos 2004: 172).

---

26 As pointed out in chapter 2, I recorded twenty-one silent moments in Group C's discussion. In fact, I interpret the participants' silence as a defiant reaction to a sense of being tested.
27 Read in this light, Yildiz's "extreme point" can be compared to what Nilüfer Göle calls "the logic of extreme emancipation, in which the body is the locus" (Göle 2010: 112).

A Question, Not Yet an Answer

No matter from what angle the participants approached LBR's performance, what remained unanswered in the discussions is the question of its aim and direction. To be more precise, it remained unclear what or who exactly represents the target of LBR's provocation.

Extract 34

(Selin): Well now I am thinking...Is this a provocation against the Turkish family or against men?
(Zeynep): It is against men in general...and also for empowering women.
(Esin): I don't think that it is against Turks.
(Zeynep): I mean in general. Women shouldn't feel inferior. You should be strong, be aware of...Well, in my opinion, she chose the wrong way to do it but that is what she says.

The attempt to determine LBR's 'real' aim caused a similar moment of doubt and indecision in Group A:

Extract 35

(Yıldız): It's just occurred to me that she is Turkish, her family and the society...but I don't think so that it is something against Turks. It's more for women. She just wants to show the power of women.
(Funda): Yes, but...
(Nisa): I'm not quite sure about that...if she really wants to demonstrate the power of women...
(Funda): *Emancipation! It's that simple! That's it!*

Group B complicated the question by adding another dimension.

Extract 36

(Berk): Well, I'm wondering...sorry for interrupting you but...well, she makes such a music video...Do you think it is against Turks or *allgemein* [general].
(Zeynep): *allgemein*, isn't it? [to me].

Rather than pinning down LBR's performance as being either against men or Turks, Berk and Zeynep suggest that it can also be understood as a broader form of provocation. As I discussed earlier, for some participants, LBR's performance defies and surpasses the limits of societal/cultural conventions in general terms, beyond distinctions made between Turkish and German culture: it is both "sittenwidrig" and "ahlak dışı." Berk and Zeynep's choice of the word "allgemein" yet again refers to society as a whole, including the dominant culture and the margin.

By wavering, pausing, critically using, venturing forth, backtracking and u-turning, the participants navigated between discourses of 'Turkish' culture, 'German' culture, and Feminism. Their shifting positionalities generated discursive turns of rhetorical borrowing and conceptual transcoding where the dichotomy of either categorical denial or radical affirmation was sidestepped.

Recognizing LBR's performance as a transgression of the boundaries that mark the cultural territory of 'Turkishness,' the participants attempted to avoid the usually available distinctions between, on the one hand, 'restricted', 'orthodox', or 'conservative', and, on the other, terms like 'emancipated', 'liberated' or 'free'. In their debate, Turkishness was unanchored and brought into motion, dislocated not only spatially and geographically, but also linguistically. That is, they invalidated the very language that positions 'Turks' in Germany as either assimilative or culturally orthodox and defensive. What remained for a now-translocally positioned Turkishness were politics of emotion of familial connections. And it is in these emotional politics where the moral boundaries and their gendered and sexed forms of embodiment are negotiated. In acts of multiple distancing, rhetorical evasion, conceptual tiptoe, offsetting of discursive edges, local unarticulation, and strategic reframing, they encountered the semantically inaccessible, the "[t]hird space of enunciation" where the language of cultural belonging became disentangled, re-entangled and brought out of joint (Bhabha 2004: 38).

Conclusion

> "But what did these phenomena *mean*? How to decide what to ask? And how to formulate questions that did not only *not* have an 'answer' per se but that problematized the conditions of interrogation in the first place?"
>
> HORTENSE J. SPILLERS, BLACK, WHITE AND IN COLOR

In the course of the group discussions, the participants' view on and self-positioning vis-à-vis LBR's performance showed unstable, and, at times, paradoxical rhetorical moves. As my study has highlighted, this instability is far from being a mere result of an inability or failure to pursue a conclusive line of arguments. Instead, the participants' hesitant, evasive, and contradictory articulations showed a careful, if not distrustful, approach to readily available sets of vocabulary, particularly regarding questions of feminist politics and its modes of embodiment. In their search for a position, or, more precisely, in their search for ways beyond the positions laid out for them *in advance*, they often ended up in discursive traps and deadlocks. Their encounter with these points of contradiction (whether they were actually met or anticipated) produced withdrawals from language as such (silences) and awkward elisions and fragmentations of the language that is available.

In fact, the building of paradoxes displayed the necessity and inevitability of failure; the very logic of how one is supposed to represent feminism in certain contexts often did not seem make sense for them. However, rather than categorically distancing themselves from LBR and her body politics, the participants looped back and forth, often revisiting their previous statements to revise and nuance their positioning. The final remarks made in Group C demonstrate this overtly:

Extract 36

(M): This is my last question. If you were students at the University of Bremen, would you attend her classes?

(Leyla): Yes, I would. Well, I'd attend her classes after watching this video too. Just only for my curiosity. Well, her lecture...well, yes, I'd attend.

(Demet): I'd like to get to know her personally too actually. I'd like to learn more about her...her opinions...the things we were thinking about her at the beginning of this discussion are so much different from what we're thinking about her now.

(Havva): Yes, that's right!

(Demet): We were too judgmental against her. And it's not what it seems to be. I'd like to know the reason. I'd definitely attend her classes.

(Havva): *Vallah* [Honestly] I agree with the others. I don't have anything to add actually...I'd also attend her classes just for my curiosity. She's different... She does something that doesn't really fit into our culture...that's why...just out of curiosity.

(Serap): Hmm...How should I put it? On the one hand, I appreciate her because...everything is not just [?]...This means she is a go-getter...I appreciate her...well...she triggers my interest...for instance...I'd also like to meet her in person.

(Demet): She acts bravely!

(Nurcan): Yes! I think she might want to give many messages. Perhaps, she wants to make the students like us listen to her. For instance, now you asked us, if we'd like to attend [her class]. Maybe it wouldn't catch my attention, if she wouldn't have done this video, perhaps I wouldn't wonder what kind of lectures she gives. To understand her worldview, to understand why she shot such a music video, I'd attend her class.

These statements show how the participants approached the complexity of LBR's performance. They conclude that LBR's feminist politics demands a closer look. That this overt withdrawal from immediate judgment occurs at the end of the discussion should, however, by no means be perceived as proving the fact that, at the end, the participants understood what LBR's performance is about, or, that they finally found something debatable, relatable or likable in it. Rather, it is a moment in which the logic of undecidability in the discussion as a whole becomes explicit. It is the moment in which that what could not be expressed manifested itself in language in the form of a metalanguage, by means of articulated self-reflection. They recognize and verbalize the need for a postponement of judgment. In other words, what the meaning of the performance eventually turns out to be, is—and cannot yet be—put into words. Since the ultimate meaning of the performance is not spelled out, it is neither categorically negated nor radically affirmed, but approached with "curiosity."

It is crucial to note that I do not suggest that the participants' movements through language and their rhetorical undecidability replicate LBR's mode of articulation, nor that the group discussions provide definite proof for the effectiveness of LBR's politics. At the same time, there are, however, parallels, if not in content, at least in form—that is, in the entanglement of certain discourses that are positioned as mutually exclusive. The participants' movement describes how they distrusted some categories and rhetorical figures yet also formed others by means of wavering and pausing, and by revisiting notions of 'Turkish culture', 'German culture', and feminism. This means, rather than a direct manifestation of a transcultural feminist discourse, the discussions show a potentiality of it. In other words, I followed the participants' shifting in between the positionalities that emerged in the course of their discussion as traces of a not-yet-existent yet becoming-sensible discourse. These speculative traces are situationally and relationally emerging, being co-constituted by the parameters of my interpretive framework. Similar to LBR's image of the 'Kanackin,' the discussions animate existing social categories towards a potential figuration of new ones. Although they showed markedly different rhetorical moves, which were, in some instances, in sharp disagreement with LBR's sexual explicitness, the discussions foregrounded a certain unreliability of claims to established positionalities, in particular regarding notions of 'Turkishness', 'Germanness', and feminism.

As I discussed in the first chapter, LBR's toying with these categories does precisely this; through contradictory statements and performative tensions, she ungrounds concepts and their production of meaning. She does this, however, not by means of radical negation, but through forms supplementation and proliferation—an affirmative politics which I call conceptual promiscuity. Embodying concepts that occupy contradictory domains, she produces transversal feminist positions that are multistable. Therefore, I argue that it is not just the use of sexual explicitness and the transgression of boundaries of political correctness per se that make her performance conceptually productive. The more interesting aspect is how she traverses different discursive fields and intertwines them so that they can make sense anew, or, at first glance, no sense at all.

In other words, in my study, LBR and my group discussion participants together animate a transcultural locational feminism as a (k)not. And this (k)not is not conceivable and articulable with pre-described notions of solidarity and allegiance. My contention is that a locational approach helps us to make sense of the politics of belonging articulated through the participants' ambiguous positioning vis-à-vis feminism. That is because a focus on locationally specific histories and dynamics in the present makes one perceptive to the positions that are not taken, even though these positions might not be directly negated and rejected.

What the participants tended to avoid as a category of identification was not feminism as such, but a certain mode of feminist embodiment that, in their view, seems to put all its stakes in so-called 'freedom' of sexual expression (bodily and rhetorically). The resulting link between explicit sexuality and notions of emancipation makes other kinds of feminism seem hopelessly uptight, orthodox, and narrow-minded. That is why it is by no means surprising that one of my group discussions was awkwardly silent. The participants withdrew from speaking since the very situation of being recorded in relation to feminism and explicit sexuality produced for them a sense of being tested for their stance on secular-modern ideals. In fact, whether in silence or through evasions and detours, the positions the participants did largely not take were those that would box them neatly into stereotypes of conservative anti-feminists, while they showed attempts to question and critique (Western feminist) notions of sexual emancipation and the kind of body politics attached to them.

The transcultural feminism incipient in their rhetorical moves unhinges primarily the concept of emancipation. Some participants remarked that emancipation for women does not necessarily have to be linked to sexual explicitness. The discussions often showed forms of epistemic disobedience that delinked established forms of making meaning of feminism and how it is supposed to be embodied. Hence their use of the term 'Sittenwidrigkeit', a concept through which they pointed out that LBR's performance reveals moral boundaries and provokes notions of tolerance beyond narrowly defined oppositions between 'Turkish culture' and 'German culture'.

As I have argued, it is in this excess where LBR turns a discourse of morality usually leveled against 'Turkish culture' against itself and stages a deliberate failure of passing. And she does this not only by means of sexual explicitness, but also through an oversignification of 'Turkishness'—rhetorically and through the inclusion of national symbols in her fashion designs. Multiplying these cultural markers, she animates a locationally specific yet nomadic feminism that is comfortably out of sync with the rhythms of belonging and representation.

My way to get in touch with the data and their interpretation, then, is grounded in an attempt to match methodologically this out-of-syncness. The analytic nodes of this study are, therefore, itself messily produced constructions that form knots of meaning that inevitably reflect the methodological setting, not just because, generally speaking, interpretation is always a process of making meaning, but also because "at the level of the 'question', a definite set of semiotic circumstances already exists, so that this question is already the beginning of an answer" (Metz 1974: 139). Thus, rather than merely aiming to dutifully, or truthfully, represent the participants' words and let them 'speak for themselves', this study embraces its own mediational function, producing a networked result that continues to make meaning as long it is involved in interpretation and evaluation. This intra-acting, self-inverted yet open-ended entanglement cannot lay claim to representation, at least not in the proper sense of the term. Like the forms of transcultural locational feminism named and described in the foregoing chapters, this study is perhaps best treated not as the last word on the matters presented, but also as a convoluted process of becoming; it is itself "not yet a code but rather [a] potential location" of "diverse possible or future codifications" (ibid: 138).

Bibliography

Adaman, Fikret/Ardıç, Oya P. (2008): "Social Exclusion in the Slum Areas of Large Cities in Turkey." In: New Perspectives on Turkey 38–39 (Spring), pp. 29–60.

Adelson, Leslie A. (1993): Making Bodies, Making History: Feminism & German Identity, Lincon and London: University of Nebraska Press.

—— (2000): "Touching Tales of Turks, Germans, and Jews: Cultural Alterity, Historical Narrative, and Literary Riddles for the 1990s." In: New German Critique 80 (April), pp. 93–124.

—— (2001a): "Against Between: A Manifesto." In: Salah Hassan/Iftikhar Dadi (eds.), Unpacking Europe: Towards a Critical Reading, Rotterdam: NAi Publishers, pp. 244–255.

—— (2005): The Turkish Turn in Contemporary German Literature: Toward a New Critical Grammar of Migration, Basingstoke and New York: Palgrave Macmillan.

—— (2011): "The Future of Futurity: Alexander Kluge and Yoko Tawada." In: The Germanic Review: Literature, Culture, Theory 86/3, pp.153–184.

Ahmed, Leila (2011): A Quiet Revolution: The Veil's Resurgence, from the Middle East to America, New Haven: Yale University Press.

Ahmed, Sara (2004): The Cultural Politics of Emotion, Edinburg: Edinburg University Press.

―――― (2012): On Being Included, Durham and London: Duke University Press.
Alexander, Jacqui/Mohanty, Chandra T. (eds.) (1997): Feminist Genealogies, Colonial Legacies, Democratic Futures, New York and London: Routledge.
Amadiume, Ifi (2003): "Bodies and Choices: African Matriarchs and Mammy Water." In: Kum Kum Bhavani (ed.), Feminist Futures: Re-Imagining Women, Culture and Development, London and New York: Zed Books, pp. 89–106.
Amelina, Anna (2012): Beyond Methodological Nationalism: Research Methodologies for Cross-Border Studies, New York and London: Routledge.
Ang, Ien (1996): "The Curse of the Smile: Ambivalence and the 'Asian' Woman in Australian Multiculturalism." In: Feminist Review, the World Upside Down: Feminisms in the Antipodes 52, pp. 36–49.
Anthias, Floya (2002): "Where Do I Belong? Narrating Collective and Translocational Positionality." In: Ethnicities 2/4, pp. 491–514.
―――― (2008): "Thinking Through the Lens of Translocational Positionality: An Intersectionality Frame for Understanding Identity and Belonging." In: Translocations: Migration and Social Change 4/1, pp. 5–20.
―――― (2012): "Hierarchies of Social Location, Class and Intersectionaltity: Towards a Translocational Frame." In: International Sociology 28/1, pp. 121–138.
Anzaldúa, Gloria (1987): Borderlands: The New Mestiza, New York: Spinsters Ink Books.
Apostolidou, Natascha (1994): "Quotierung Für Migrantinnen-Eine Ambivalente, Aber Notwendige Forderung." In: Cornelia Eichhorn/Sabine Grimm (eds.), Gender Killer: Texte Zu Feminismus Und Politik, Berlin-Amsterdam: Edition ID-Archiv, pp. 65–69.
Appadurai, Arjun (1996): Modernity Al Large: Cultural Dimensions of Globalization, Minneapolis: University of Minnesota Press.

Arslan, Savas (2010): Cinema in Turkey: A New Critical History, Oxford: Oxford University Press.

Auer, Peter (2002a): "Introduction: Bilingual Conversation Revisited." In: Peter Auer (ed.), Code-Switching in Conversation: Language, Interaction and Identity, New York and London: Routledge, pp. 1–24.

――― (2002b): Code-Switching in Conversation: Language, Interaction and Identity, New York and London: Routledge.

――― (2007): "The Monolingual Bias in Biligualism Research, or: Why Bilingual Talk is (still) a Challange for Linguistics." In: Monica Heller (ed.), Bilingualism: A Social Approach, Basingstoke and New York: Palgrave Macmillan, pp. 319–339.

Aulenbacher, Brigitte/Meuser, Michael/Riegraf, Birgit (2010): Soziologische Geschlechterforschung: Eine Einführung, Wiesbaden: VS Verlag für Sozialwissenschaft.

Ayim, May (1997): Grenzenlos Und Unverschämt, Berlin: Orlanda.

Badawia, Tarek (2002): Der Dritte Stuhl, Berlin: Iko-Verlag.

Bailey, Benjamin (2007): "Heteroglossia and Boundaries." In: Monica Heller (ed.), Bilingualism: A Social Approach, Basingstoke and New York: Palgrave Macmillan, pp. 257–276.

Bal, Mieke/ Á Hernández-Navarro, Miguel (eds.) (2011): Art and Visibility in Migratory Culture: Conflict, Resistance, and Agency, Amsterdam and New York: Rodopi Press.

Bamberg, Michael G. W. (2003): "Positioning with Davie Hogan: Stories, Tellings, and Identities." In: Colette Daiute (ed.), Narrative Analysis: Studying the Development of Individuals in Society, Thousand Oaks and London: SAGE, pp. 135–159.

Barad, Karen (2001): "Re(con)figuring Space, Time, Matter." In: Marianne DeKoven (ed.), Feminist Locations: Global and Local, Theory and Practice, New Brunswick and New Jersey: Rutgers University Press, pp. 75–109.

――― (2007): Meeting the Universe Halfway: Quantum Physics and the Entanglement of Matter and Meaning, Durham and London: Duke University Press.

——— (2010): "Quantum Entanglements and Hauntological Relations of Inheritance: Dis/ Continuities, Spacetime Enfoldings, and Justice-to-Come." In: Derrida Today 3/2, pp. 240–268.

——— (2012a): "Matter Feels Converses Suffers Desires Yearns and Remembers": Interview with Karen Barad." In: Rick Dolphijn/Iris van der Tuin (eds.), New Materialisms: Interviews & Cartographies, Open Humanities, Press June 1, 2013 (http://quod.lib.umich.edu/o/ohp/11515701.0001.001/1:4.3/--new-materialism-interviews-cartographies?rgn=div2;view=fulltext), pp. 48–70.

——— (2012b): "On Touching—The Inhuman That Therefore I Am." In: Differences 23/3, pp. 206–23.

Barbour, Rosaline (2008): Doing Focus Groups, Thousand Oaks and London: SAGE.

Becker, Ruth/Kortendiek, Beate (2010): Handbuch Frauen- und Geschlechterforschung: Theorie, Methoden, Empirie, 3rd ed., Wiesbaden: VS Verlag für Sozialwissenschaft.

Beer, David (2014): Punk Sociology, Basingstoke and New York: Palgrave Macmillan.

Behar, Ruth (2003): Translated Woman: Crossing the Border with Esperanza's Story, Boston: Beacon Press.

Benhabib, Seyla (1995): Feminist Contentions: A Philosophical Exchange, New York and London: Routledge.

——— (2002): The Claims of Culture—Equality and Diversity in Global Era, New Jersey: Princeton University Press.

Berlant, Lauren (2011): Cruel Optimism, Durham and London: Duke University Press.

Bhabha, Homi K. (1994): The Location of Culture, London: Taylor & Francis Press.

——— (2004): The Location of Culture, 2nd ed., New York and London: Routledge.

Bhambra, Gurminder K. (2009): Rethinking Modernity: Postcolonialism and the Sociological Imagination, Basingstoke and New York: Palgrave Macmillan.

Bhatia, Tej K./Ritchie, William C. (eds.) (2013): The Handbook of Bilingualism and Multilingualism, 2nd ed., New Jersey: Wiley-Blackwell Publishing.
Bhavani, Kum Kum (2005): Feminist Futures: Re-Imagining Women, Culture and Development, London and New York: Zed Books.
Birks, Melanie/Mills, Jane (2011): Grounded Theory: A Practical Guide, Los Angeles: SAGE.
Blau, Judith R./Brown, Eric S. (2001): "Du Bois and Diasporic Identity: The Veil and the Unveiling Project." In: Sociological Theory 19/2, pp. 219–33.
Bloor, Michael (2001): Focus Groups in Social Research, London: SAGE.
Borgstrom, Michael (2006): "Face Value: Ambivalent Citizenship in Iola Leroy." In: African American Review 40/4, pp. 779.
Borsò, Vittoria (2007): Transkulturation: literarische und mediale Grenzräume im deutsch-italienischen Kulturkontakt, Bielefeld: transcript Verlag.
Brah, Avtar (1996): Cartographies of Diaspora: Contesting Identities, 1st ed., New York and London: Routledge.
Braidotti, Rosi (1994): Nomadic Subjects: Embodiment and Sexual Difference in Contemporary Feminist Theory, Columbia: Columbia University Press.
——— (2013): Nomadic Theory: The Portable Rosi Braidotti, Columbia: Columbia University Press.
Brooks, Ann (2002): Postfeminisms: Feminism, Cultural Theory and Cultural Forms, New Yotk and London: Routledge.
Budgeon, Shelle. (2001): "Emergent Feminist(?) Identities: Young Women and the Practice of Micropolitics." In: European Journal of Women's Studies 8/1, pp. 7–28.
Bulbeck, Chilla (1998): Re-Orienting Western Feminisms: Women's Diversity in a Postcolonial World, Cambridge: Cambridge University Press.

Bundesministeriums der Justiz (2013): Bürgerliches Gesetzbuch (BGB), May 16, 2014 (http://www.gesetze-im-internet.de/bgb/index.html).

Busch, Brigitta (2012): "The Linguistic Repertoire Revisited." In: Applied Linguistics 33/5, pp. 503–23.

Butler, Judith (1990): Gender Trouble: Feminism and the Subversion of Identity, New York and London: Routledge.

——— (1993): Bodies That Matter: On the Discursive Limits of Sex, New York: Psychology Press.

Bütow, Birtgit (2011): "Gender Trotz(t) Entgrenzung? Anayzsen Zu Jugend, Alter Und Gesclecht." In: Elke Kleina et al. (eds.), Ambivalente Erfahrungen: (Re-)politisierung der Geschlechter, Opladen and Farmington Hills: Verlag Barbara Budrich, pp. 31–45

Büyük Türkçe Sözlük Online (Great Turkish Dictionary Online) 22 May, 2013 (http://www.tdk.gov.tr/index.php?option=com_bts).

Canning, Kathleen (2006): Gender History in Practice: Historical Perspectives on Bodies, Class & Citizenship, Ithaca and New York: Cornell University Press.

Casale, Rita/Gerhard, Ute/Wischerman, Ulla (2008): "Einleitung: Neuer Feminismus?" In: Femininistische Studien 2 (November), pp. 9.

Chakrabarty, Dipesh (2009): Provincializing Europe: Postcolonial Thought and Historical Difference, Princeton: Princeton University Press.

Charmaz, Kathy (2000): "Grounded Theory Objectivist and Constructivist Methods." In: Norman K. Denzin/Yvonna S. Lincoln (eds.), The SAGE Handbook of Qualitative Research, 2nd ed., Thousand Oaks: SAGE, pp. 509–536.

——— (2006): Constructing Grounded Theory: A Practical Guide Through Qualitative Analysis, Thousand Oaks: SAGE.

Chin, Rita (2007): The Guest Worker Question in Postwar Germany, Cambridge: Cambridge University Press.

——— (2010): "Turkish Women, West German Feminists, and the Gendered Discourse on Muslim Cultural Difference." In: Public Culture 22 /3, pp. 557-581.

Clarke, Adele E. (2005): Situational Analysis: Grounded Theory After the Postmodern Turn, Thousand Oaks: SAGE.

——— (2007): "Grounded Theory: Critiques, Debates, and Situational Analysis." In: William Outhwaite/Stephen Turner (eds.), The SAGE Handbook of Social Science Methodology, Thousand Oaks and London: SAGE, pp. 423–443.

Coleman, Rebecca/Ringrose, Jessica (2013): "Introduction: Deleuze and Research Methodologies." In: Rebecca Coleman/Jessica Ringrose (eds.), Deleuze Connections: Deleuze and Research Methodologies, Edinburg: Edinburgh University Press, pp. 1–22.

Collins, Patricia H. (2000): Black Feminist Thought: Knowledge, Consciousness, and the Politics of Empowerment, New York and London: Routledge.

Corbin, Juliet M/Strauss, Anselm L. (2008): Basics of Qualitative Research: Techniques and Procedures for Developing Grounded Theory, Thousand Oaks and London: SAGE.

Darowska, Lucyna/Lüttenberg, Thomas/Machold, Claudia (2010): Hochschule Als Transkultureller Raum?: Kultur, Bildung Und Differenz in Der Universität, 1st ed., Bielefeld: transcript Verlag.

Davidson, Joyce/Bondi, Liz/ Smith, Mick (2007): Emotional Geographies, Farnham and Burlington: Ashgate.

De Carteau, Michel (1980): "'Spaces' and 'Places.'" In: Claire Doherty (ed.), Situation, London: Whitechapel Gallery, pp. 118–120.

DeKoven, Marianne (ed.) (2001): Feminist Locations: Global and Local, Theory and Practice, New Brunswick and New Jersey: Rutgers University Press.

Deleuze, Gilles (1994): Difference and Repetition, translated by Paul Patton, Columbia: Columbia University Press.

Denzin, Norman K. (2007): On Understanding Emotion, New Brunswick and New Jersey: Transaction Publishers.

——— (2010): The Qualitative Manifesto: A Call to Arms, California: Left Coast Press.
Denzin, Norman K./ Lincoln, Yvonna S. (2003): Collecting and Interpreting Qualitative Materials, New York and London: SAGE.
Derrida, Jacques (1981): Positions, translated by Alan Bass and Henri Ronse, Chicago: University of Chicago Press.
——— (1998a): Of Grammatology translated by Gayatri Chakravorty Spivak, Baltimore: Johns Hopkins University Press.
——— (1998b): Monolingualism of the Other: Or, the Prosthesis of Origin, Standford: Stanford University Press.
Der Spiegel (1995): "Agitpop Aus Dem Ghetto.", April 24, 2010 (http://www.spiegel.de/spiegel/print/d-9181199.html).
De Sousa Santos, Boaventura (2004): "A Critique of Lazy Reason: Against the Waste of Experience'." In: Immanuel Maurice Wallerstein (ed.), The Modern World-System in the Longue Durée, Boulder: Paradigm Publishers, pp. 157–197.
——— (2013): "Topology: Epistemologies of the South - Part 2.", 24 June, 2014 (http://www.tate.org.uk/context-comment/video/topo logy-epistemologies-south-part-2).
Dirim, İnci/ Hieronymus, Andreas (2003): "Cultural Orientation and Language Use among Multilingual Youth Groups: 'For Me It Is like We All Speak One Language.'" In: Journal of Multilingual and Multicultural Development 24/1-2, pp. 42–55.
Dirlik, Arif (1998): The Postcolonial Aura: Third World Criticism in the Age of Global Capitalism, Boulder: Westview Press.
Dorn, Thea (2006): Die neue F-Klasse: wie die Zukunft von Frauen gemacht wird, München and Zürich: Verlag Piper.
Du Bois, W. E. B. (1903): The Souls of Black Folk, edited by Brent Hayes Edwards, New York: Oxford University Press.
"Duisburg-Marxloh: Ghetto oder Integration." (2010): Livestream, Spiegel TV, December 18, 2011 (http://www.spiegel.tv/filme/ duisburg-marxloh/).

Dussel, Enrique D. (1999): The Underside of Modernity: Apel, Ricoeur, Rorty, Taylor, and the Philosophy of Liberation, edited by Eduardo Mendieta, Amherst and New York: Humanity Book.

Edwards, John (2013): "Bilingualism and Multilingualism: Some Central Concepts." In: Tej K. Bhatia/William C. Ritchie (eds.), The Handbook of Bilingualism and Multilingualism, New Jersey: Wiley-Blackwell Publishing, pp. 5–25.

Ehrkamp, Patricia (2013): "'I've Had It with Them!' Younger Migrant Women's Spatial Practices of Conformity and Resistance." In: Gender, Place & Culture 20/1, pp. 19–36.

Eichhorn, Cornelia/ Grimm, Sabine (eds.) (1995): Gender Killer: Texte zu Feminismus und Politik, Berlin and Amsterdam: Edition ID-Archiv.

Eismann, Sonja (2007): Hot Topic: Popfeminismus heute. 2nd ed., Mainz: Ventil Verlag.

Elger, Katrin (2008): "Meine Zeit Wird Kommen." In: Der Spiegel, 22 March, 2010 (http://www.spiegel.de/spiegel/print/d-562990 96.html).

Engel, Antke (1999): "Queer-Feministische Und Kanakische Angriffe Auf Die Nation." In: Vor Der Information, pp. 2–5.

Enzenhofer, Edith/Resch, Katharina (2011): "Übersetzungsprozesse und deren Qualitätssicherung in der qualitativen Sozialforschung." In: Forum Qualitative Sozialforshung/ Forum: Qualitative Social Research 12/2, Art. 10, September 19, 2016 (http://www.qualitative-research.net/index.php/fqs/article/view/1652/3177).

Fairclough, Norman (1995): Critical Discourse Analysis: The Critical Study of Language, London and New York: Longman.

——— (1999): "Linguistic and Intertextuality Analysis within Discourse Analysis." In: Nikolas Coupland/Adam Jaworski (eds.), The Discourse Reader, New York and London: Routledge, pp. 183–212.

——— 2003): Analysing Discourse: Textual Analysis for Social Research, New York and London: Routledge.

Faludi, Susan (1992): Backlash: The Undeclared War Against Women, New York: Random House.

Fanon, Frantz (1967): A Dying Colonialism, New York: Grove Press.

FeMigra (1995): "Wir, die Seiltänzerinnen Politische Strategien von Migrantinnen gegen Ethnisierung und Assimilation." In: Cornelia Eichhorn/Sabine Grimm (eds.), Gender Killer: Texte zu Feminismus und Politik, pp. 49–64.

Ferree, Myra (2012): Varieties of Feminism: German Gender Politics in Global Perspective, Standford: Stanford University Press.

Fina, Anna De/ Schiffrin, Deborah/Bamberg, Michael (2006): Discourse and Identity, Cambridge: Cambridge University Press.

Fox, Nick J./Alldred, Pam (2014): "New Materialist Social Inquiry: Designs, Methods and the Research-Assemblage." In: International Journal of Social Research Methodology, 26 June, 2014 (doi:10.1080/13645579.2014.921458), pp 1–16.

Gabaccia, Donna R. (1994): From the Other Side: Women, Gender, and Immigrant Life in the U.S., 1820-1990, Bloomington: Indiana University Press.

Garcia Canclini, Nestor (2005): Hybrid Cultures: Strategies For Entering And Leaving Modernity. Translated by Christopher L. Chiappari and Silvia L. Lopez, Minneapolis: University of Minnesota Press.

Geerts, Evelien/van der Tuin, Iris (2013): "'From Intersectionality to Interference: Feminist onto-Epistemological Reflections on the Politics of Representation.'" In: Women's Studies International Forum 45, pp. 171–178.

Geertz, Clifford (1983): Local Knowledge: Further Essays in Interpretive Anthropology, New York: Basic Books.

Gelbin, Cathy S./Konuk, Kader/Piesche, Peggy (1999): AufBrüche: kulturelle Produktionen von Migrantinnen, Schwarzen und jüdischen Frauen in Deutschland, Frankfurt am Main: Ulrike Helmer Verlag.

Genz, Stéphanie/Brabon, Benjamin A. (2009): Postfeminism: Cultural Texts and Theories, Edinburg: Edinburgh University Press.

Gerhard, Ute (1999): Atempause: Feminismus als demokratisches Projekt, Frankfurt am Main: Fischer Taschenbuch Verlag.

Gill, Rosalind/Scharff, Christina (2013): New Femininities: Postfeminism, Neoliberalism and Subjectivity, Basingstoke and New York: Palgrave Macmillan.

Gilroy, Paul (1993): "Between Afro-Centrism and Euro-Centrism: Youth Culture and the Problem of Hybridity." In: Young: Nordic Journal of Youth Research 1/2, pp. 2–13.

―――― (2010): Darker Than Blue: On the Moral Economies of Black Atlantic Culture, Cambridge: Harvard University Press.

Glaser, Barney G./Strauss, Anselm L. (1967): The discovery of grounded theory: strategies for qualitative research, New York: Aldine Publishing Company.

Go, Julian (2013): "For a Postcolonial Sociology." In: Theory and Society 42, pp. 25–55.

Göktürk, Deniz/Grambling, David/Kaes, Anton (eds.) (2007): "The Turks are coming! Save yourself if you can!" In: Germany in transit: nation and migration, 1955-2005, translated by David Grambling, 110–111, Berkeley: University of California Press.

Göle, Nilüfer (1996): The Forbidden Modern: Civilization and Veiling, Michigan: University of Michigan Press.

―――― (2000): "Global Expectations, Local Experiences: Non-Western Modernities." In: Arts, Wilhelmus Antonius (ed.), Through a Glass, Darkly: Blurred Images of Cultural Tradition and Modernity over Distance and Time, Leiden; Boston and Tokyo: Brill Press, pp. 40–55

―――― (2010): "European Self-Presentation and Narratives Challenged by Islam: Secular Modernity in Question." In: Gutiérrez Rodríguez, Encarnación/ Boatcă, Manuela/ Costa, Sérgio (eds.), Decolonizing European Sociology: Transdisciplinary Approaches, Farnham and Burlington: Ashgate, pp. 103–115.

―――― (2011): Islam in Europe: the lure of fundamentalism and the allure of cosmopolitanis. Princeton and New Jersey: Markus Wiener Publishers.

González y González, Elsa M./ Lincoln, Yvonne (2006): "Decolonizing Qualitative Research: Non-Traditional Reporting Forums in the Academy." In: Forum Qualitative Sozialforshung/ Forum: Qualitative Social Research 7/4, Art. 1, April, 16 (2011http://nbn-resolving.de/urn:nbn:de:0114-fgs060418).

Greenbaum, Thomas L. (2000): Moderating Focus Groups: A Practical Guide for Group Facilitation, Thousand Oaks; London: SAGE.

Griffin, Christine (1989): "'I'm Not a Women Libber, but...': Feminism, Consciousness and Identity." In: Skevington, Suzanne/ Baker, Deborah (eds.), The Social Identity of Women, Thousand Oaks and London: SAGE, pp. 173–193.

Gullberg, Marianne (2013): "Bilingualism and Gesture." In: Bhatia, Tej K./ Ritchie, William C (eds.), The Handbook of Bilingualism and Multilingualism, New Jersey: Wiley-Blackwell Publishing, pp. 417–438.

Gültekin, Neval (1986): "Anpassung Zur Emanzipation?" In: Beiträge Zur Feministische Theorie Und Praxis 9/18, pp. 92–94.

Gümen, Sedef (1994): "Geschlecht Und Ethnizität in Der Bundesdeutschen Und US-Amerikanischen Fraunforschung." In: Texte Zur Kunst 15 (September), pp 127–139.

——— (1996): "Sie Sozialpolitische Konstruktion 'Kultureller' Differenzen in Der Bundesdeutschen Frauen- Und Migrationsforshung." In: Beiträge Zur Feministische Theorie Und Praxis. Entfremdung: Migration und Dominanzgesellschaft 42/19, pp. 77–89.

——— (2007): "Das Soziale des Geschlecht: Frauenforschung und die Kategorie 'Ethnizität.'" In: Hark, Sabine (ed.), Dis/Kontinuitäten: Feministische Theorie, Wiesbaden: VS Verlag für Sozialwissenschaften, pp. 145–163.

Gutiérrez Rodríguez, Encarnación (1996a): "Migratinnenpolitik Jenseits Des Differenz- Und Identitätsdiskurses." In: Beiträge Zur Feministische Theorie Und Praxis. Ent-fremdung: Migration und Dominanzgesellschaft 42/19, pp. 99–111.

—— (1996b): "Frau ist nicht gleich Frau, nicht gleich Frau, nicht gleich Frau ... Über die Notwendigkeit einer kritischen Dekonstruktion in der feministischen Forschung." In: Fischer, Ute L./Kampshoff, Marita / Keil, Susanne/ Schmitt, Mathilde (eds.), Kategorie: Geschlecht?, Geschlecht und Gesellschaft 6, Wiesbaden: VS Verlag für Sozialwissenschaften, pp. 163–190.

—— (1999a): Intellektuelle Migrantinnen - Subjektivitäten im Zeitalter von Globalisierung: eine postkoloniale dekonstruktive Analyse von Biographien im Spannungsverhältnis von Ethnisierung und Vergeschlechtlichung, Opladen: Leske und Budrich Verlag.

—— (1999b): Intellektuelle Migrantinnen – Subjektivitäten Im Zeitalter von Globalisierung, Opladen: Leske und Budrich Verlag.

—— (1999c): "Akrobik in der Marginalitaet. Zur Produktionsbedingungen intellektueller Frauen im Kontext der Arbeitmigration." In: Gelbin, Cathy S/Konuk, Kader/Piesche, Peggy (eds.), AufBrüche: kulturelle Produktionen von Migrantinnen, Schwarzen und jüdischen Frauen in Deutschland, Frankfurt am Main: Ulrike Helmer Verlag, pp. 207–223.

—— (1999d): "Fallstricke des Feminismus. Das Denken 'kritischer Differenzen' ohne geopolitische Kontextualisierung. Einige Überlegungen zur Rezeption antirassistischer und postkolonialer Kritik." In: Polylog: Zeitschrift für interkulturelles Philosophieren 4, pp. 13–24.

—— (2001a): "Vergesellschaftung revisited?! Das konkave Glas der Konstitution und Konstruktion. Strategien der Dekonstruktuion und postkoloniale Kritik am institutionellen Feminismus." In: Gümen, Sedef/ Hornung, Ursula/Weilandt, Sabine (eds.), Zwischen Emanzipationsvision und Gesellschaftskritik: (Re)Konstruktionen der Geschlechterordnung in Frauenforschung, Frauenbewegung, Frauenpolitik, Münster: Westfälisches Dampfboot, pp 135–151.

—— (2001b): "Widerstand in Différance: Repraesentation, Vereinnahmung Und Gegenstrategien von MigrantInnen Und Schwarzen Deutschen." In: Informationszentrums 3. Welt, 253 (June), pp. 22–23.

—— (2003): "Repräsentation, Subalternität und postkoloniale Kritik." In: Steyerl, Hito/Gutiérrez Rodríguez, Encarnación (eds.), Spricht die Subalterne deutsch?: Migration und postkoloniale Kritik, Münster: Unrast Verlag, pp. 17–37.

—— (2004): "Transversales Übersetzen als dekonstruktive Verstehenspraxis in den Gender Studies." In: Helduser, Urte/Marx, Daniela/
Paulitz, Tanja/Pühl, Katharina (eds.), Under construction?: konstruktivistische Perspektiven in feministischer Theorie und Forschungspraxis, Frankfurt am Main and New York: Campus Verlag, pp. 195–207.

—— (2006): "Translating Positionality On Post-Colonial Conjunctures and Transversal Understanding." In: Eipcp European Institute for Progressive Cultural Policies, June 15, 2009 (http://eipcp. net/transversal/0606/gutierrez-rodriguez/en).

—— (2008): "'Lost in Translation' - Transcultural Translation and Decolonialization of Knowledge." Translated by Camilla Nielsen and Shirley Anne Tate, June 15, 2009 (http://eipcp.net/transver sal/0608/gutierrez-rodriguez/en).

—— (2010a): "Transculturation in German and Spanish Migrant and Diasporic Cinema: On Constrained Spaces and Minor Intimacies in Princesses and A Little Bit of Freedom." In: Berghahn, Daniela/Sternberg, Claudia (eds.), European Cinema in Motion Migrant and Diasporic Film in Contemporary Europe, Basingstoke and New York: Palgrave Macmillan, pp. 114–131.

—— (2010b): "Decolonizing Postcolonial Rhetoric." In: Gutiérrez Rodríguez, Encarnación/Boatcă, Manuela/Costa, Sérgio (eds.), Decolonizing European Sociology: Transdisciplinary Approaches, Farnham and Burlington: Ashgate, pp. 49–67.

— (2010c): "Postkolonialismus: Subjektivität, Rassismus und Geschlecht." In: Becker, Ruth/Kortendiek Beate (eds.), Handbuch Frauen- und Geschlechterforschung: Theorie, Methoden, Empirie, 3rd ed., Wiesbaden: VS Verlag für Sozialwissenscahft, pp. 274–282.

— (2010d): Migration, Domestic Work and Affect: A Decolonial Approach on Value and the Feminization of Labor, New York and London: Routledge.

— (2010): "'My Traditional Clothes Are Sweat-Shirts and Jeans'. Über die Schwierigkeit, nicht different zu sein oder Gegen-Kultur als Zurichtung.", July 14, 2011 (http://eipcp.net/transversal/0101/gutierrezrodriguez/de).

Gutiérrez Rodríguez, Encarnación/Boatcă, Manuela/Costa, Sérgio (eds.) (2010): Decolonizing European Sociology: Transdisciplinary Approaches, Farnham and Burlington: Ashgate.

Gwynne, Joel (2013): Erotic Memoirs and Postfeminism: The Politics of Pleasure, Basingstoke and New York: Palgrave Macmillan.

Halberstam, J. Jack (2012): Gaga Feminism: Sex, Gender, and the End of Normal, Boston: Beacon Press.

Hall, Stuart. (1997): Representation: Cultural Representations and Signifying Practices, Thousand Oaks and London: SAGE

— (1998): "What Is This Black Inn 'Black' Popular Culture?." In: Dent, Gina (ed.), Black Popular Culture, Seattle: Bay Press, pp. 465–475.

Hall, Stuart/du Gay, Paul (eds): (1996): Questions of Cultural Identity, London: SAGE.

Harding, Sandra (2008): Sciences from Below: Feminisms, Postcolonialities, and Modernities, Durham and London: Duke University Press.

Hark, Sabine (2007): Dis/Kontinuitäten: Feministische Theorie, Wiesbaden: VS Verlag für Sozialwissenschaften.

Harvey, David (2000): Spaces of Hope, Berkeley: University of California Press.

Hausbacher, Eva/Klaus, Elisabeth/Poole, Ralph/ Brandl, Ulrike/Schmutzhart, Ingrid (2012): Migration und Geschlechterverhältnisse: Kann die Migrantin sprechen?, Wiesbaden: VS Verlag für Sozialwissenschaften.

Heller, Monica (ed.) (2007a.): Bilingualism: A Social Approach, Basingstoke and New York: Palgrave Macmillan.

—— (2007b): "Bilingualims as Ideology and a Practice." In: Heller, Monica (ed.), Bilingualism: A Social Approach, Basingstoke and New York: Palgrave Macmillan, pp. 1–24.

Henwood, Karen/ Griffin, Christine/Phoenix, Ann (1998): Standpoints and Differences: Essays in the Practice of Feminist Psychology, Thousand Oaks and London: SAGE.

Hernández, Daisy/Rehman, Bushra (2002): Colonize This!: Young Women of Color on Today's Feminism, New York: Seal Press.

Herrmann, Steffen Kitty (2005): "Queer(e) Gestalten. Praktiken der Derealisierung von Geschlecht." In: Haschemi Yekani, Elahe/Michaelis, Beatrice (eds.), Quer Durch Die Geisteswissenschaften: Perspektiven Der Queer Theory, Berlin: Quer Verlag, pp. 53–72.

Herzing, Evi/Plesch, Hans/Engelmann, Jonas/ Plesch, Tine/Melián, Michaela (eds.) (2013): Rebel Girl: Popkultur und Feminismus, 1st ed., Mainz: Ventil Verlag.

Hess, Sabine/Langreiter, Nikola/Timm, Elisabeth (2011): Intersektionalität Revisited: Empirische, Theoretische Und Methodische Erkundungen, 1st ed., Bielefeld: transcript Verlag.

Hooks, Bell (1990): Yearning: Race, Gender, and Cultural Politics, Boston: South End Press.

—— (1994): Outlaw Culture: Resisting Representations, New York and London: Routledge.

Hornung, Ursula/Gümen, Sedef/Weilandt, Sabine (2001): Zwischen Emanzipationsvision und Gesellschaftskritik: (Re)Konstruktionen der Geschlechterordnung in Frauenforschung, Frauenbewegung, Frauenpolitik, Münster: Westfälisches Dampfboot.

Hügel, Ika/Lange, Chris/Ayim, May/a.o. (eds.) (1999): Entfernte Verbindungen: Rassismus, Antisemitismus, Klassenunterdrückung, 2nd ed., Berlin: Orlanda Frauenverlag.

Huq, Rupa (2006): Beyond Subculture: Pop, Youth And Identity In A Postcolonial World, New York and London: Routledge.

Jankie, Dudu (2004): "'Tell Me Who You Are': Problematizing the Construction and Positionalities of 'Insider'/'Outsider' of a 'Native' Ethnographer in a Postcolonial Context." In: Mutua, Kagendo/ Beth Blue Swadener (eds.), Decolonizing Research in Cross-Cultural Contexts: Critical Personal Narratives, Albany: SUNY Press, pp. 87–105.

Jaworski, Adam (1997): Silence: Interdisciplinary Perspectives, Berlin: Walter de Gruyter.

Jaworski, Adam/Coupland, Nikolas (1999): The Discourse Reader, New York and London: Routledge.

Jolles, Marjorie, (2012): "Going Rogue: Postfeminism and the Privilege of Breaking Rules." In: Feminist Formations 24/3, pp. 43–61.

Kallmeyer, Werner/ Keim, Inken (2003): "Linguistic Variation and the Construction of Social Identity in a German-Turkish Setting: A Case Study of an Immigrant Youth Group in Mannheim, Germany." In: Androutsopoulos, Jannis K./Georagakopoulou, Alexandra (eds.), Discourse Constructions of Youth Identities, Amsterdam: John Benjamins Publishing, pp. 29–46.

Karakaşoğlu, Yasemin (2003): "Custom Tailored Islam? Second Generation Female Students of Turko-Muslim Origin in Germany and Their Concept of Religiousness in the Light of Modernity and Education." In: Sackmann, Rosemarie/Peters, Bernhard/Faist, Thomas (eds.), Identity and Integration: Migrants in Western Europe, Farnham and Burlington: Ashgate

Kauer, Katja (2009): Popfeminismus! Fragezeichen!: Eine Einführung, 1st ed., Berlin: Frank & Timme.

Keim, Inken (2007): Die "türkischen Powergirls": Lebenswelt und kommunikativer Stil einer Migrantinnengruppe in Mannheim, Tübingen: Narr Francke Attempto Verlag.

Keller, Reiner (2013): Doing Discourse Research: An Introduction for Social Scientists. Thousand Oaks and London: SAGE.

Kirchner, Stephanie (2008): "German Feminism: Playing Dirty." In: Time, June 26, 2010 (http://content.time.com/time/magazine/article/0,9171,1815720,00.html).

Kitzinger, Jenny (1994): "The Methodology of Focus Groups: The Importance of Interaction between Research Participants." In: Sociology of Health & Illness 16/1, pp. 103–121.

Kitzinger, Jenny/Barbour, Rosaline (1999): Developing Focus Group Research: Politics, Theory and Practice, Thousand Oaks and London: SAGE.

Knapp, Gudrun-Axeli, (1988): "Die Vergessene Differenz." In: Hark, Sabine (ed.), Dis/Kontinuitäten: Feministische Theorie, Wiesbaden: VS Verlag für Sozialwissencahft, pp. 263–284.

——— (2005): "Race, Class, Gender: Reclaiming Baggage in Fast Travelling Theories." In: European Journal of Women's Studies 12/3, Thousand Oaks and London: SAGE, pp. 249-65.

——— (2007): "Entschiedene Interventionen in der Unentscheidbarkeit. Von queerer Identitätsktirik zur VerUneindeutigung als Methode." In: Hark, Sabine (ed.), Dis/Kontinuitäten: Feministische Theorie, Wiesbaden: VS Verlag für Sozialwissencahft, pp. 285–304.

——— (2008): "Verhältnisbestimmungen: Geschlect, Klasse, Ethnizität." In: Klinger, Cornelia/Knapp, Gudrun-Axeli (eds.), ÜberKreuzungen: Fremdheit, Ungleichheit, Differenz, Münster: Westfälisches Dampfboot, pp. 138–170.

——— (2012): Im Widerstreit: Feministische Theorie in Bewegung, Wiesbaden: VS Verlag für Sozialwissencahft.

Korobov, Neill (2001): "Reconciling Theory with Method: From Conversation Analysis and Critical Discourse Analysis to Positioning Analysis." In: Forum Qualitative Sozialforshung/ Forum:

Qualitative Social Research 2/3 September 21, 2016 (http://www.qualitative-research.net/index.php/fqs/article/view/906).

Kovner, Sarah (2012): Occupying Power: Sex Workers and Servicemen in Postwar Japan, Standford: Standford University Press.

Krueger, Richard A. (1997): Moderating Focus Groups, Thousand Oaks and London: SAGE.

――― (1998): Developing Questions for Focus Groups, Thousand Oaks and London: SAGE.

Krueger, Richard A./Casey, Mary Anne (2000): Focus Groups: A Practical Guide for Applied Research, Thousand Oaks and London: SAGE.

Laclau, Ernesto (1996): Emancipation(s), London and New York: Verso.

Ladner, Joyce A. (1998): The Death of White Sociology: Essays on Race and Culture, Baltimore: Black Classic Press.

Lady Bitch Ray (2006): "Keine ist so krass wie ich", October 25, 2008 (http://www.taz.de/1/archiv/?id=archivseite&dig=2006/07/03/a0108).

――― (2009): "Bin nicht deutsch, nicht türkisch, bin 'ne Kanackin!", October 25, 2008 (http://www.bild.de/unterhaltung/leute/lady-bitch-ray/lady-bitch-ray-in-neuer-bild-serie-6146894.bild.html).

――― (2012a): "Ich bin ein moralischer Mensch.", October 25, 2013 (http://www.taz.de/1/archiv/digitaz/artikel/?ressort=ku&dig=2012/01/28/a0031).

――― (2012b): Bitchsm: Emanzipation, Integration, Masturbation, Stuttgart: Panini Verlags.

――― (2013): Dr. Sahin und Lady Bitch Ray im Doppel-Interview: Die Frau mit den zwei Seelen, October 25, 2014 (http://www.bild.de/regional/bremen/lady-bitch-ray/lady-reyhan-sahin-interview-32468800.bild.html).

――― (2014): Ich kann meine Wut nur durch diese Sexualisierung ausdrücken, April 23, 2014 (http://www.tagesanzeiger.ch/leben/

gesellschaft/Ich-kann-meine-Wut-nur-durch-diese-Sexualisie
rung-ausdruecken/story/16511302).
Lady Bitch Ray bei Schmidt und Pocher, (2008), November 15, 2009 (http://www.youtube.com/watch?v=uwWBIXNyfqA&feature=yo utube_gdata_player).
Leavy, Patricia (2014): "A Brief Statement on the Public and the Future of Qualitative Research." In: Leavy, Patricia (ed.), The Oxford Handbook of Qualitative Research, Oxford and New York: Oxford University Press, pp. 724–731.
Lees, Sue (1986): Losing Out: Sexuality and Adolescent Girls, Lodnon: Hutchinson.
Liamputtong, Pranee (2011): Focus Group Methodology: Principle and Practice, Thousand Oaks and London: SAGE.
Lincoln, Yvonna S./Denzin, Norman K. (2003): "Introduction: Revolutions, Ruptures, and Rifs in Interpretive Inquiry." In: Lincoln, Yvonna S./Denzin, Norman K. (eds.), Turning Points in Qualitative Research: Tying Knots in the Handkerchief 3, Walnut Creek, AltaMira Press, pp. 1–16.
Lübcke, Claudia (2007): "Jugendkulturen Junger Muslime in Deutschland." In: von Wensierski, Hans-Jürgen/Lübcke, Claudia (eds.), Junge Muslime in Deutschland—Lebenslangen, Aufwachsprozesse Und Jugendkulturen, Opladen and Farmington Hills: Verlag Barbara Budrich, pp. 285–319.
Lutz, Helma (1999): "Sind wir uns immer noch fremd- Konstruktionen von Fremdheit in Weissen Frauenbewegung." In: Hügel, Ika/Lange, Chris/Ayim, May, a.o. (eds.), Entfernte Verbindungen: Rassismus, Antisemitismus, Klassenunterdrückung, 2nd ed., Berlin: Orlanda Frauenverlag, pp. 138–156.
Lykke, Nina (2012): "Intersectional Analysis: Black Box or Useful Critical Feminist Thinking Technology?" In: Lutz, Helma/ Herrera Vivar, Maria Teresa/Supik, Linda (eds.), Framing Intersectionality: Debates on a Multi-Faceted Concept in Gender Studies, Farnham and Burlington: Ashgate, pp. 207–220.

Macswan, Jeff (2013): "Code-Switching and Grammatical Theory." In: Bhatia, Tej K./Ritchie, William C. (eds.), The Handbook of Bilingualism and Multilingualism, New Jersey: Blackwell Publishing, pp. 323–350.

Mae, Michiko (2007): "Auf Dem Weg Zu Einer Transkulturellen Genderforschung." In: Mae, Michiko/Saal, Britta (eds.), Transkulturelle Genderforschung: Ein Studienbuch zum Verhältnis von Kultur und Geschlecht, Wiesbaden: VS Verlag für Sozialwissenschaften, pp. 37–51.

Mahmood, Saba (2005): Politics of Piety: The Islamic Revival and the Feminist Subject, Princeton: Princeton University Press.

Massumi, Brian (2002): Parables for the Virtual: Movement, Affect, Sensation, Durham and London: Duke University Press.

McGoey, Linsey (2012): "Strategic Unknowns: Towards a Sociology of Ignorance." In: Economy and Society 41/1, pp. 1–16.

McRobbie, Angela (2009): The Aftermath of Feminism: Gender, Culture and Social Change, Thousand Oaks and London: SAGE.

——— (2011): "Beyond Post-Feminism." In: Public Policy Research 18/3, pp. 179–184.

Mecheril, Paul (2003): Politik der Unreinheit ein Essay über Hybridität, Wien: Passagen-Verlag.

Metz, Christian (1974): Language and Cinema, Berlin: Walter de Gruyter.

Mignolo, Walter D. (2007): "Delinking." In: Cultural Studies 21/2, pp. 449–514.

——— (2009): "Epistemic Disobedience, Independent Thought and De-Colonial Freedom." In: Theory, Culture, and Society 26/7-8, pp. 1–23.

——— (2011): The Darker Side of Western Modernity: Global Futures, Decolonial Options, Durham and London: Duke University Press.

——— (2012): Local Histories/Global Designs: Coloniality, Subaltern Knowledges, and Border Thinking, Princeton: Princeton University Press.

Minnaard, Liesbeth (2008): New Germans, New Dutch: Literary Interventions, Amsterdam: Amsterdam University Press.

Mirandé, Alfredo (1981): La Chicana: The Mexican-American Woman, Chicago: University of Chicago Press.

Mitchell, Tony (2001): Global Noise: Rap and Hip-Hop Outside the USA, Middletown: Wesleyan University Press.

Modleski, Tania (1991): Feminism Without Women: Culture and Criticism in a "Postfeminist" Age, New York and London: Routledge.

Mohanty, Chandra Talpade (n.d): "'Under Western Eyes' Revisited: Feminist Solidarity through Anticapitalist Struggle." In: Signs: Journal of Women in Culture and Society 28/2, pp. 499–536.

Moraga, Cherríe/ Anzaldúa, Gloria (1983) This Bridge Called My Back: Writings by Radical Women of Color, New York: Kitchen Table, Women of Color Press.

Mörchen, Stefan (2011): Schwarzer Markt: Kriminalität, Ordnung und Moral in Bremen 1939-1949, Frankfurt am Main: Campus Verlag.

Morgan, David L. (1997): Focus Groups as Qualitative Research. Thousand Oaks and London: SAGE.

——— (1998): Planning Focus Groups, Thousand Oaks and London: SAGE.

Morgan, Joan (1999): When Chickenheads Come Home to Roost: A Hip-Hop Feminist Breaks It Down, New York: Simon & Schuster Paperbacks.

Morton, Stephen (2004): Gayatri Chakravorty Spivak, London and New York: Routledge.

Nilan, Pam/Feixa, Carles (2006): Global Youth?: Hybrid Identities, Plural Worlds, London and New York: Routledge.

Niranjana, Tejaswini (1992): Siting Translation History, Post-Structuralism, and The Colonial Context, Berkeley: University of California Press.

Nold, Christian (ed.) (2009): "Emotional Cartography: Technologies of the Self", September 21, 2016 (http://www.emotionalcartography.net/EmotionalCartography.pdf).

Oguntoye, Katharina/Ayim, May (1986): Farbe bekennen: afrodeutsche Frauen auf den Spuren ihrer Geschichte, Frankfurt am Main: Fischer Verlag.

Otyakmaz, Berrin Özlem (1995): Auf allen Stühlen: Das Selbstverständnis junger türkischer Migrantinnen in Deutschland, Köln: ISP Verlag.

——— (1999): "'Und die denken dann von vornherein, das läuft irgendwie ganz anders ab' Selbst- und Fremdbilder junger Migrantinnen türkischer Herkunft." In: Beiträge Zur Feministische Theorie Und Praxis 22/51, pp. 79–92.

Owusu, Kwesi (2000): Black British Culture and Society: A Text Reader, New York: Psychology Press.

Özdamar, Emine Sevgi (2000): Life Is a Caravanserai: Has Two Doors I Came in One I Went Out the Other, London: Middlesex University Press.

"Oxford English Dictionaries Online", May 22, 2013 (http://www.oxforddictionaries.com/).

Palenga-Möllenbeck, Ewa (2009): "Die Unsichtbaren ÜbersetzerInnen in der transnationalen Forschung." In: Lutz, Helma (ed.), Gender Mobil?: Geschlecht Und Migration in Transnationalen Räumen, 1st ed., Münster: Westfälisches Dampfboot, pp. 158–173.

Pecheux, Michel (1986): Language, Semantics and Ideology: Stating the Obvious, Basingstoke and New York: Palgrave Macmillan.

Peglow, Katja/ Engelmann, Jonas Engelmann (2013): Riot Grrrl Revisited!: Geschichte und Gegenwart einer feministischen Bewegung, 2nd ed., Mainz: Ventil Verlag.

Phoenix, Ann (2006): "Interrogating Intersectionality: Productive Ways of Theorising Multiple Positioning." In: Kvinder, Køn & Forskning 2-3, pp. 21–30.

Poland, Blake/ Pederson, Ann (1998): "Reading Between the Lines: Interpreting Silences in Qualitative Research." In: Qualitative Inquiry 4/2, pp. 293–312.

Ponzanesi, Sandra (2011): "Europe in Motion: Migrant Cinema and the Politics of Encounter." In: Social Identities 17/1, pp. 73–92.

Potter, Russell A. (1995): Spectacular Vernaculars: Hip-Hop and the Politics of Postmodernism, Albany: SUNY Press.

Prümm, Kathrin/Sackmann, Rosemarie/Shultz, Tanjev (2003): "Collective Identities of Turkish Migrants in Germany--The Aspect of Self-Localization." In: Sackmann, Rosemarie/Peters, Bernhard/Faist, Thomas (eds.), Identity and Integration: Migrants in Western Europe, Farnham and Burlington: Ashgate, pp. 161–170.

Puar, Jasbir K. (2007): Terrorist Assemblages: Homonationalism in Queer Times, Durham and London: Duke University Press.

Pusch, Barbara (2001): Die neue muslimische Frau: Standpunkte & Analysen, Würzburg: Ergon-Verlag.

Puwar, Nirmal (2004): Space Invaders Race, Gender and Bodies out of Place, Oxford and New York: Berg Press.

Räthzel, Nora (1999): "Hybridität ist die Antwort, aber was war noch mal die Frage?" In: Kossek, Brigitte (ed.), Gegen-Rassismen. Konstruktionen - Interaktionen - Interventionen, Hamburg: Argument, pp. 204–219.

――― (2010): "Rassismustheorien: Geschlechterverhältnisse und Feminismus." In: Becker, Ruth/Kortendiek, Beate (eds.), Handbuch Frauen- und Geschlechterforschung: Theorie, Methoden, Empirie, 3rd ed., Wiesbaden: VS Verlag für Sozialwissencahft, pp. 283–291.

Reuter, Julia/ Villa, Paula Irene (2008): Postkoloniale Soziologie: Empirische Befunde, theoretische Anschlüsse, politische Intervention, Bielefeld: transcript Verlag.

Roche, Charlotte/Busch, Liz (2001): Charlotte Roche und Liz Busch: "Ohne dich wäre ich nicht ich." August 12, 2009 (http://www.emma.de/artikel/charlotte-roche-und-liz-busch-ohne-dich-waere-ich-nicht-ich-263884).

Roth, Hans-Joachim/Terhart, Henrike/Anastasopoulos, Charis (2012): Sprache und Sprechen im Kontext von Migration: Worüber man sprechen kann und worüber man (nicht) sprechen soll, Wiesbaden: Springer Verlag.

Said, Edward W. (1978): Orientalism, London: Penguin Books India.

Sakai, Naoki (2012): "Positions and Positionalities: After Two Decades." In: Positions 20/1, pp. 67–94.

Saldaña, Johnny (2009): The Coding Manual for Qualitative Researchers, London and New York: SAGE.

Savage, Jon (2011): England's Dreaming, London: Faber & Faber.

Scharff, Christina (2013): "The New German Feminisms: Of Wetlands and Alpha-Girls." In: Gill, Rosalind/Scharff, Christina (eds.), New Femininities: Postfeminism, Neoliberalism and Subjectivity, Basingstoke and New York: Palgrave Macmillan, pp. 279–292.

Schwarzer, Alice (2005): "Editorial von Alice Schwarzer: Wir Sind Kanzlerin!" In: EMMA, March 6, 2011 (http://www.emma.de/artikel/editorial-von-alice-schwarzer-wir-sind-kanzlerin-263194).

Scollon, Ron/Scollon, Suzanne B. K. (2012): Intercultural Communication: A Discourse Approach, New Jersey: Wiley-Blackwell Publishing.

Şenocak, Zafer (2000): Atlas of a Tropical Germany: Essays on Politics and Culture, 1990-1998, translated by Leslie A. Adelson, Nebreska: University of Nebraska Press.

Sifianou, Maria (1997): "Silence and Politeness." In: Jaworski, Adam (ed.) Silence: Interdisciplinary Perspectives, Berlin: Walter de Gruyter, pp. 63–84.

Skeggs, Beverley (1993): "Two Minute Brother: Contestation through Gender, 'race' and Sexuality." In: Innovation: The European Journal of Social Science Research 6/3, pp. 299–322.

——— (1997): Formations of Class & Gender: Becoming Respectable, Thousand Oaks and London: SAGE.

Smith, Linda Tuhiwai (1999): Decolonizing Methodologies Research and Indigenous Peoples, London: Zed Books, pp. 1-18.

Smith, Michael Peter (2011): "Translocality: A Critical Reflection." In: Brickell, Katherine/Datta, Ayona (eds.), Translocal Geographies: Spaces, Places, Connections, Farnham and Burlington: Ashgate, pp. 182–198.

Smithson, Janet (2000): "Using and Analysing Focus Groups: Limitations and Possibilities." In: International Journal of Social Research Methodology 3/2, pp. 103–119.

Soja, Edward W. (1989): Postmodern Geographies: The Reassertion of Space in Critical Social Theory, London and New York: Verso.

——— (1996): Thirdspace: Journeys to Los Angeles and Other Real-and-Imagined Places, New Jersey: Wiley Blackwell Publishing.

——— (2010): Seeking Spatial Justice, Minneapolis: University of Minnesota Press.

Sökefeld, Martin (2008): Struggling for Recognition: The Alevi Movement in Germany and in Transnational Space, Oxford and New York: Berghahn Books.

Spiers, Emily (2012): "'Alpha-Mädchen Sind Wir Alle': Subjectivity, Agency and Solidarity in Anglo-American and German Popfeminist Writing." In: Angermion 5/1, pp. 191–218.

Spillers, J. Hortense (2003): Black, White and in Color: Essays on American Literature And Culture, Chicago: University of Chicago Press.

Spivak, Gayatri Chakravorty (1988): "Can the Subaltern Speak?" In: Nelson, Cary/Grossberg, Lawrence (eds.), Marxism and the Interpretation of Culture, Champaign: University of Illinois Press, pp. 271–313.

——— (1998): "Translator's Preface." In: Of Grammatology, ix – lxxxix, Baltimore: Johns Hopkins University Press.

——— (2000): "Translation as Culture." In: Parallax 6/1, pp. 13–24.

Springer, Kimberly (2007): "Divas, Evil Black Bitches, and Bitter Black Women: African American Women in Postfeminist and Post-Civil-Rights Popular Culture." In: Tasker, Yvonne/Negra, Diane (eds.), Interrogating Postfeminism: Gender and the Politics of Popular Culture, Durham and London: Duke University Press, pp. 249-267.

Stanford Friedman, Susan (1998): Mappings—Feminism and the Cultural Geographies of Encounters, Princeto: Princenton University Press.

——— (2001): "Locational Feminism: Gender, Cultural Geographies, and Geopolitical Literacy." In: DeKoven, Marianne (ed.), Feminist Locations: Global and Local, Theory and Practice, New Brunswick and New Jersey: Rutgers University Press, pp. 13–36.

Stehle, Maria (2011): "Pop, Porn, and Rebellious Speech." In: Feminist Media Studies 12/2, pp. 229–247.

——— (2012): Ghetto Voices in Contemporary German Culture: Textscapes, Filmscapes, Soundscapes, Rocherster and New York: Camden House.

Stets, Jan E./Turner, Jonathan H. (eds.) (2006): Handbook of the Sociology of Emotions, New York: Springer.

Steyerl, Hito (1994): Deuschland und das Ich, Berlin: VHS. Short-documentary.

——— (2001): "Ornamente Der Neuen Mitte: Wo Widerstand Zu Kanak-Chic Wird." In: Informationszentrums 3. Welt, 253 (June), pp. 24–26.

——— (2004): "Gaps and Potentials: The Exhibition 'Heimat Kunst': Migrant Culture as an Allegory of the Global Market." In: New German Critique, 92 (April), pp. 159–168.

Steyerl, Hito/Gutiérrez Rodríguez, Encarnación (eds.) (2003): Spricht die Subalterne deutsch?: Migration und postkoloniale Kritik, Münster: Unrast Verlag.

Strauss, Anselm L./Corbin; Juliet M. (1994): "Grounded Theory Methodology - An Overview." In: Denzin, Norman K./Lincoln, Yvonna S. (eds.), The SAGE Handbook of Qualitative Research, 1st ed., Thousand Oaks and London: SAGE, pp. 273–285.

——— (1997): Grounded Theory in Practice, Thousand Oaks and London: SAGE.

Stroud, Christhoper (2007): "Bilingualims: Colonialism and Postcolonialism." In: Heller, Monica (ed.), Bilingualism: A Social Approach, Basingstoke and New York: Palgrave Macmillan, pp. 25–49.

Swadener, Beth Blue/ Mutua, Kagendo (2004): "Afterword." In: Swadener, Beth Blue/ Mutua, Kagendo (eds.), Decolonizing Research in Cross-Cultural Contexts: Critical Personal Narratives, Albany: SUNY Press, pp. 255–261.

Tasker, Yvonne/Negra, Diane (2007): Interrogating Postfeminism: Gender and the Politics of Popular Culture, Durham and London: Duke University Press.

Tate, Shirley (2012): "Michelle Obama's Arms: Race, Respectability, and Class Privilege." In: Comparative American Studies 10/2-3, pp. 226–238.

Tawada, Yoko (2010): Abenteuer der deutschen Grammatik: Gedichte, Tübingen: Claudia Gehrke Verlag.

Taylor, Charles (2002): "Modern Social Imaginaries." In: Public Culture 14/1, pp. 91–124.

Taylor, Jill McLean (1997): Between Voice and Silence: Women and Girls, Race and Relationship, Cambridge: Harvard University Press.

"The Disruptive Visibility of Islam in European Publics. 2011." September 9, 2012 (http://www.youtube.com/watch?v=HZ1tXX3 yEGw&feature=youtube_gdata_player).

Thomas, Greg (2006): Proud Flesh Inter/Views: Sylvia Wynter in ProudFlesh: A New African Journal of Culture, Politics & Consciousness, Issue 4.

Thomas, Greg (2009): Hip-Hop Revolution in the Flesh: Power, Knowledge, and Pleasure in Lil' Kim's Lyricism, Basingstoke and New York: Palgrave Macmillan.

Tomlinson, Barbara (2013): "Colonizing Intersectionality: Replicating Racial Hierarchy in Feminist Academic Arguments." In: Social Identities 19/2, pp. 254–272.

Tuider, Elisabeth (2009): "Transnationales Erzählen. Zum Umgang Mit Über-Setzungen in Der Biografieforschung." In: Lutz, Helma (ed.), Gender Mobil?: Geschlecht Und Migration in Transnationalen Räumen, 1st ed., Münster: Westfälisches Dampfboot, pp. 174–192.

———— (2011): "'Sitting at a Crossroads' Methodisch einholen: Intersektionalität in Der Perspektive Der Biographieforschung." In: Hess, Sabine/Langreiter, Nikola/Timm, Elisabeth (eds.), Intersektionalität Revisited: Empirische, Theoretische Und Methodische Erkundungen, 1st ed., Bielefeld: transcript Verlag, pp. 221–246.

Tuzcu, Pinar (2012): "Performing Female 'Kanackness'--Transcultural Perpectives on Lady Bitch Ray." In: Bütow, Birgit/Kahl, Ramona/Stach, Anna (eds.), Körper, Geschlecht, Affekt: Selbstinszenierungen und Bildungsprozesse in Jugendlichen Sozialräumen, Wiesbaden: VS Verlag für Sozialwissenscahft, pp. 157–173.

———— (2013): "'Diese Bitch Ist Eine Gefahr' Lady Bitch Ray and the Dangerous Supplement. A Transcultural Locational Feminist Reading." In: Hawel, Marcus (ed.), WORK IN PROGRESS. WORK ON PROGRESS. Doktorand_innen-Jahrbuch 2012 Der Rosa-Luxemburg-Stiftung, Hamburg: VSA-Verlag, pp. 203–216.

Tuzcu, Pinar/Motzek, Sina (2013): "Kulturelle Übersetzung– Perspektiverweiterung Und Irritation in Mehrsprachiger Migrationsforschung." In: Esen, Erol/Borde, Theda (eds.), Deutschland und die Türkei – Band II. Forschen, Lernen und Zusammenarbeiten in Gesellschaft, Gesundheit und Bildung, Ankara: Siyasal Kitabevi, pp. 368-380.

Vargas-Silva, Carlos (2012): Handbook of Research Methods in Migration, Cheltenham, and Northampton: Edward Elgar Pub.

Venuti, Lawrence (1998): The Scandals of Translation: Towards an Ethics of Difference, New York and London: Routledge.

———— (2000): The Translation Studies Reader, New York and London: Routledge.

Villa, Paula-Irene, (2009): "'Liebeslieder waren gestern': Zur Jugendschutzproblematik von Porno- und Gansterrap.", December 23, 2010 (http://www.kjm-online.de/files/pdf1/Villa.pdf).
Villa, Paula-Irene/Jäckel, Julia/Pfeiffer, Zara S./Steckert, Ralf/ Sanitter, Nadine (2012): Banale Kämpfe?, Wiesbaden: Springer Verlag.
Volkmann, Maren (2011): Frauen und Popkultur: Feminismus, Cultural Studies, Gegenwartsliteratur, Bochum: Posth Verlag.
Walgenbach, Katharina (2007): Gender als interdependente Kategorie: neue Perspektiven auf Intersektionalität, Diversität und Heterogenität, Opladen and Farmington Hills: Verlag Barbara Budrich.
Warner, Michael (1993): Fear of a Queer Planet: Queer Politics and Social Theory, Minneapolis: University of Minnesota Press.
Weheliye, Alexander G. (2014): Habeas Viscus: Racializing Assemblages, Biopolitics, and Black Feminist Theories of the Human. Durham and London: Duke University Press.
Wei, Li (2011): "Moment Analysis and Translanguaging Space: Discursive Construction of Identities by Multilingual Chinese Youth in Britain." In: Journal of Pragmatics 43 (December), pp. 1222–1235.
——— (2013): "Conceptual and Methodological Issues in Bilingualism and Multilingualism Research." In: Bhatia, Tej K./ Ritchie, William C. (eds.), The Handbook of Bilingualism and Multilingualism, New Jersey: Wiley-Blackwell Publishing, pp. 26–52.
Welsch, Wolfgang (1994): "Transculturality the Puzzling Form of Cultures Today." In: California Sociologist, 17 & 18, pp. 194–213.
Werbner, Pnina/Modood, Tariq (1997): Debating Cultural Hybridity: Multi-Cultural Identities and the Politics of Anti-Racism, London and New York: Zed Books.
White, Jenny B. (1997): "Turks in the New Germany." In: American Anthropologist 99/4, pp. 754–769.

Williams, Simon (2000): Emotion and Social Theory: Corporeal Reflections on the (Ir) Rational, Thousand Oaks and London: SAGE.
Yildiz, Yasemin (1999): "Keine Adresse in Deutschland?" In: Gelbin, Cathy S./Konuk, Kader/Piesche, Peggy (eds.), AufBrüche: kulturelle Produktionen von Migrantinnen, Schwarzen und jüdischen Frauen in Deutschland, Frankfurt am Main: Ulrike Helmer Verlag, pp. 224–237.
––––––– (2004): "Critically 'Kanak': A Reimagination of German Culture." In: Gardt, Andreas/Hüppauf, Bernd (eds.), Globalization and the Future of German, Berlin: Mouton de Gruyter, pp. 319–340.
––––––– (2011): "Governing European Subjects: Tolerance and Guilt in the Discourse of 'Muslim Women.'" In: Cultural Critique 77/1, pp. 70–101.
––––––– (2012): Beyond the Mother Tongue: The Postmonolingual Condition, New York: Fordham University Press.
––––––– (2013): "Response on Forum 'Translation and Migration.'" In: Translation Studies 6/1, pp. 103–107.
Yuval-Davis, Nira (1997): "Ethnicity, Gender Relations and Multiculturalism." In: Werbner, Pnina/Modood, Tariq (eds.), Debating Cultural Hybridity Multi-Cultural Identities and the Politics of Anti-Racism, London and New York: Zed Books, pp. 193–209.

IMAGES CITED

Image 1: Lay Bitch Ray official webside, (http://www.lady-bitch-ray.com/txbl/lady-ray-fotos/?album=2&gallery=4).

Image 2: Screenshot from a talk show program *Markuz Lanz* (16.06.2011), August 8, 2013) (http://www.zdf.de/ZDFmediathek/beitrag/video/1362080/Markus-Lanz-vom-16.-Juni-2011#/hauptnavigation/startseite).

Image 3: Screen shot from the documentary *A German Mind with a Turkish Heart* (2009), dir. Murat Seker.

Image 4: Cover image of *Mobil das Maganizevon Deutsche Bahn,* June, 2014.

Image 5: *Ein Interview mit Charlotte Roche und Liz Busch*: „Ohne dich wäre ich nicht ich".

September 10, 2012 (http://www.emma.de/artikel/charlotte-roche-und-liz-busch-ohne-dich-waere-ich-nicht-ich-263884).

Image 6: Lay Bitch Ray official webside, (http://www.lady-bitch-ray.com/tx-bl/lady-ray-fotos/?album=2&gallery=4).

Image 7: Lay Bitch Ray official webside, (http://www.lady-bitch-ray.com/tx-bl/lady-ray-fotos/?album=2&gallery=4).

Image 8: Lay Bitch Ray official webside, (http://www.lady-bitch-ray.com/tx-bl/lady-ray-fotos/?album=2&gallery=4).

Social Sciences

Maik Fielitz, Laura Lotte Laloire (eds.)
Trouble on the Far Right
Contemporary Right-Wing Strategies
and Practices in Europe

2016, 208 p., 19,99 € (DE),
ISBN 978-3-8376-3720-5
E-Book: 17,99 € (DE), ISBN 978-3-8394-3720-9
EPUB: 17,99 € (DE), ISBN 978-3-7328-3720-5

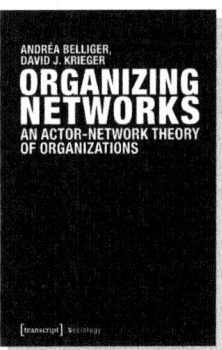

Andréa Belliger, David J. Krieger
Organizing Networks
An Actor-Network Theory of Organizations

2016, 272 p., 34,99 € (DE),
ISBN 978-3-8376-3616-1
E-Book: 34,99 € (DE), ISBN 978-3-8394-3616-5

Julia Sattler (ed.)
Urban Transformations in the U.S.A.
Spaces, Communities, Representations

2016, 426 p., 39,99 € (DE),
ISBN 978-3-8376-3111-1
E-Book: 39,99 € (DE), ISBN 978-3-8394-3111-5

All print, e-book and open access versions of the titels in our entire list
are available in our online shop www.transcript-verlag.de/en!

Social Sciences

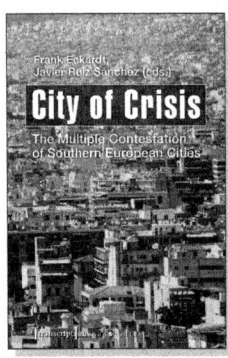

Frank Eckardt, Javier Ruiz Sánchez (eds.)
City of Crisis
The Multiple Contestation
of Southern European Cities

2015, 264 p., 29,99 € (DE),
ISBN 978-3-8376-2842-5
available as free open access publication
E-Book: ISBN 978-3-8394-2842-9

Derya Özkan (ed.)
Cool Istanbul
Urban Enclosures and Resistances

2014, 172 p., 29,99 € (DE),
ISBN 978-3-8376-2763-3
E-Book: 26,99 € (DE), ISBN 978-3-8394-2763-7

Michael Friedman, Samo Tomsic (eds.)
Psychoanalysis: Topological Perspectives
New Conceptions of Geometry and Space
in Freud and Lacan

2016, 256 p., 34,99 € (DE),
ISBN 978-3-8376-3440-2
E-Book: 34,99 € (DE), ISBN 978-3-8394-3440-6

All print, e-book and open access versions of the titels in our entire list
are available in our online shop www.transcript-verlag.de/en!